"With *The Complete DVD Book*, Gore & Salamoff win the Oscar for best book for the independent filmmaker."

— Bob Jones, Teacher/Filmmaker
University of Central Florida

"This book ushers in the Age of Empowerment for independent filmmakers who have enough entrepreneurial spirit to take charge of their own careers. Chris Gore's legendary status as an outlaw of Hollywood offers readers an opportunity to keep their street credibility while following his coherent plan to capture a share of the fastest growing market in the industry today."

— Catherine Clinch, Contributing Editor,
Creative Screenwriting Magazine

"Both thorough and to the point, *The Complete DVD Book* is a great investment of time and money."

– Jason Tenenbown, Senior Producer,
"NCAA DVD Trivia Challenge"
(Interactive DVD)

THE COMPLETE
DVD
BOOK

DESIGNING, PRODUCING, AND MARKETING YOUR INDEPENDENT FILM ON DVD

CHRIS GORE & PAUL J. SALAMOFF

Published by Michael Wiese Productions
11288 Ventura Blvd., Suite 621
Studio City, CA 91604
Tel. 818.379.8799
Fax 818.986.3408
mw@mwp.com
www.mwp.com

Cover Design: Michael Wiese Productions
Layout: Gina Mansfield
Editor: Paul Norlen

Printed by McNaughton & Gunn, Inc., Saline, Michigan
Manufactured in the United States of America

Library of Congress Cataloging-in-Publication Data

Gore, Chris, 1965-
  The complete DVD book : producing, marketing & selling your
independent film on DVD / Chris Gore and Paul J. Salamoff.
      p. cm.
   ISBN 1-932907-09-2
  1. Motion pictures--Production and direction. 2. Motion
pictures--Marketing. 3. DVD-Video discs. 4. Independent filmmakers.
I. Salamoff, Paul J., 1971- II. Title.
   PN1995.9.P7G66 2005
   791.4302'32--dc22

                                    2005009462

Table of Contents

Acknowledgments

The authors would like to thank the following people and organizations for their valuable assistance in the preparation of this book.

First of all this book would not exist without the tireless work of my writing partner Paul J. Salamoff. He is due special thanks for trusting me to move forward on this project, and for writing all the sections that contain the technical mumbo-jumbo that I still do not completely grasp. I'm just not a technical person I guess.

The following people helped along the way whether they were aware of it or not — Mark Bell, Mitchell Bard, Eric Campos, Stephen Gates, Phil Hall, Gadi Harel, Geoff Leavitt, David Fritz and David Shapiro of Niche Media Ventures, Scott Miller, and all the filmmakers from Film Threat DVD. And finally, thanks to my lovely wife Marion for all her support for the crazy projects I am passionate about. Thank you.

— *Chris Gore*

A special thanks to Jaime Levy for her vast knowledge on the technology of DVDs, Jerry Hsu from Apple Inc. for "hooking me up" with the new software, my manager Scott Karp for continuing to believe in me no matter what nutty directions my career takes me, my best friends Bill Zahn, Garrick Dion, and Stephen Susco for always being there for me when I needed a boost of confidence, my parents Edward and Susan for teaching me that anything is possible, and finally my wife Melissa and daughter Samantha for all their support and love.

— *Paul J. Salamoff*

Introduction

THE INDEPENDENT DVD REVOLUTION

The tremendous success of DVD has dramatically changed the film business. In addition to new releases, studios can dump their libraries of old films onto the digital format and release them to consumers hungry for their favorite films from the past. DVD has become so important to the major studios' bottom line that separate production crews follow filmmakers from the beginning of the process through every step to gather content for those all-important DVD extra features. New DVD releases reach store shelves with the kind of fanfare often reserved for theatrical premieres.

This versatile digital format has not only become the electronics product most rapidly adopted by mainstream consumers, it has also created a significant additional revenue stream for movie studios. Studios have quickly learned that even if a film bombs at the box office, greater rewards can be seen once the film comes out on DVD. Those titles often reach store shelves within six months of the theatrical release and go on to see profits higher than those from movie ticket sales. It is not an exaggeration to say that the DVD has saved the studios. In fact, 2001 was the first year in which DVD sales eclipsed the total box office take of all films released to theaters. With this fact in mind, the time is ripe for a revolution in independent film. And the answer lies in three little letters: D-V-D.

These shiny discs have created new opportunities for emerging filmmakers to have their work discovered. More than 2,000 independent features are produced each year. Of those, only a lucky 100 or so find modest theatrical distribution, with the rest left unseen and without a home. DVD offers a chance for filmmakers whose movies may have been lost in the shuffle to find new life. Filmmakers now have the power to release their movies independently through this exciting and affordable new medium.

Filmmakers are not only distributing their films on DVD themselves or through small independent DVD labels, they're seeing something they probably never expected — profits. This "DIY" or do-it-yourself approach to releasing a DVD is happening more and more frequently and with even greater success. Manufacturing and authoring costs have become so cheap that practically anyone can become their own DVD distributor. With a run of 1,000 DVDs, an indie might pay $2.50 or less per unit including packaging. For filmmakers who are frustrated by distributors who lack vision, self-distribution or distribution through a small distributor is now a viable option. Selling those 1,000 DVDs through a website could potentially net an indie an $18,000 profit. Not bad when most of these films have budgets under $100,000. Even modest sales of a DVD can turn a small independent film into a break-even proposition, which puts the movie ahead of most of those big studio pictures making it to theaters.

In the following pages you will learn almost nothing about screenwriting, directing or filmmaking. There are plenty of other books on those topics. What this book does explain is a no-bullshit, soup-to-nuts approach to producing, authoring, marketing, selling, and finally, releasing your project on DVD.

Because the authors of this book worked on various sections separately, you may notice two distinct voices addressing issues throughout these pages. Whenever the subject is technical, addressing the nuts and bolts side of DVD production, you're reading Paul. And whenever the subject involves sales, marketing, or inspirational tidbits, you're reading Chris. The wealth of information necessary to successfully release your film on DVD required a two-headed monster, so please excuse the shifting tones. Both Chris and Paul are well-versed in their respective areas of expertise, so when it comes to the ins and outs of DVD, you're getting a full course meal prepared by two cooks.

Enjoy.

Keep one final thing in mind as you sift through this mountain of information. Ultimately, you are asking someone — a buyer either from a video store or a film fan — to spend money on your DVD. Put yourself in their shoes for a moment. Whether the issue involves package design or menu architecture or bonus features or a clever marketing hook, you are asking someone to plunk down money to buy or rent your film. So get into the heads of avid DVD viewers and every choice you make in completing your project will become that much easier.

Section 1

BEFORE YOU START

WHY RELEASE YOUR INDEPENDENT FILM ON DVD?

Timing is everything in the film business. Perhaps you are one of the 95% of filmmakers who have shopped your film around to distributors and not found any takers. Or maybe you've got a few deals on the table, but not exactly the right one. A filmmaker who has a completed project now has two choices:

1. — Sell to a distributor who will release the DVD.

2. — Self-distribute on DVD.

Before choosing one of these two options, an independent filmmaker must have exhausted all other options. To get to the point where you've decided to self-distribute your film, you should either have screened at film markets or played at film festivals. Both outlets serve to introduce your film to buyers.

The purpose of the film festival circuit is to promote your movie, gathering reviews and feedback that will be used in the marketing of the feature. The best time to consider a commercial release is after your film has completed at least one year of festival screenings. If in that year your film has not been picked up for distribution, then you will want to weigh other options to make money on your film such as self-distributing and releasing your film on DVD.

There are two main reasons to release your movie on DVD. One reason is to make money. Many independent filmmakers say, "You know, I just want to get it out there." As an indie filmmaker, you deserve to make money on your investment. And there is significant money to be made, especially if the film has been made on a low budget. For example, if you have made your film for under $100,000, the possibility of making a profit or at least breaking even through a domestic DVD release is within reach. Making a cable TV sale to, say, the Independent Film Channel or HBO is another possibility. Combine a domestic DVD release and cable sale with a few international sales and you can actually make a profit on a small independent film.

The second, and most important, reason to release your film on DVD is to promote your career as a filmmaker. You spent all this time making a movie; at the very least the result should be the beginnings of your film career. Sure, anyone can burn a DVD of their movie, but a film on DVD in commercial release proves that your talents as a filmmaker have won the approval of the marketplace. Now you can walk into a meeting and pro-claim, "Here is a copy of my movie on DVD, please watch it." The DVD becomes in effect a showcase of your talents as a filmmaker. A commercial release also gives you legitimacy as a filmmaker — it means that audiences have accepted your film as a product. Filmmakers hate to hear this, but in the world of commercial release, films are ultimately "products." This is a depressing truth but filmmakers need to come to grips with this fact.

An added benefit of releasing your film on DVD is to experience some sort of completion for the project. A lot of filmmakers I know will have a movie that plays the festival circuit and kind of makes the rounds but is never officially released. Until a film is officially released, it's almost as if the film remains incomplete. A DVD acts as a final record that is left for future audiences to see.

TO SUCCEED IN THE FILM BUSINESS

In order to be successful as a filmmaker you need to balance the left side (logical) and the right side (creative) of your brain. You have to be incredi-bly creative to be successful as a filmmaker. On the other hand, you also have to be a very savvy businessperson. Generally a creative mind and a business mind don't gel in the same skull. You either need to partner with really smart people (generally other producers) that can make up for the skills that you lack, or you need to develop those skills for yourself. Balancing your creative side and your business side is critical.

It's no secret that some of the most successful filmmakers are also very savvy business people. In fact, the most successful filmmaker on the planet is very savvy and that's Steven Spielberg. Love him or hate him, Spielberg is a very intelligent businessman as well as a very creative filmmaker from the standpoint that his films touch so many people. (This also moves people to touch their wallets to shell out money for tickets and DVDs.) Spielberg's movies have a very broad appeal. But he wouldn't be nearly as successful if he weren't such a successful businessperson. So the challenge for you is to balance those two sides. You don't necessarily want one side to take over the other. If you're too business-minded, you're going to end up with some lame, commercial crap that will appeal to everyone, that is, no one. And if you focus solely on the creative and ignore the business side, you'll find it very hard to keep making films. Filmmakers that are serious about their careers learn to balance the business and the creative aspects of the game.

CHOOSING SELF-DISTRIBUTION — ADVANTAGES AND DISADVANTAGES

If you're thinking of self-distributing your movie there are several advantages and disadvantages to carefully weigh. Many filmmakers feel that self-distribution is freedom. It *can* be, but you need to consider a couple of things before you think of self-distribution as the way to go for yourself:

Do you have the time?

Can you balance all the things necessary to successfully self-distribute your movie along with your current daily activities, as it can quickly become a full-time job?

Do you have the talents and skills necessary to successfully distribute your own film?

Can you spend the next two years squeezing as much money as you can out of this movie, or should you make another film?

Frankly, self-distribution for filmmakers is a very tough road and I would recommend it only for those with skills that go beyond filmmaking. Aside from the fact that there are all kinds of hidden marketing costs that go with reaching significant unit sales numbers, I believe distribution is best left to those with the expertise to get it done, mainly those with marketing and sales experience. It's true that some things are best delegated to people better equipped to do their jobs. And many believe that *filmmakers should make movies* and *distributors should distribute movies.*

However, if you are a filmmaker who really wants to have control and looks at every single dollar carefully, perhaps self-distribution *is* for you. You will certainly have control over every single facet of your DVD. Keep in mind that every aspect includes: the authoring, the design, the replication, the marketing, the sales, the packaging, the distribution, the accounting, the shipping, and the managing of all the outlets that the film is sold through. Self-distribution gives you complete control over how your film is sold in the marketplace.

Self-distribution can also limit you, so you need to weigh all the requirements. The experience can be a sense of freedom combined with the weight of an awesome responsibility. Self-distribution should be viewed as a last resort for a filmmaker. I think that most filmmakers are better off partnering with a small distributor than they are self-distributing. Self-distributing should really be your last choice on the road to getting your film released.

The primary challenge facing filmmakers who choose the route of self-distribution is this — you're only dealing with *one* film. You are shipping *one* DVD to a video store, you're shipping *one* film to a retailer. There's no incentive for these outlets to pay you what they owe you. As someone who has a small company that distributes movies on DVD, we're constantly in a position where we haven't been paid for the last film that we sent, so we hold the next title hostage. And we tell our retail outlets, "Hey, you need to pay us for the last movie before we send you the next movie." Because we have a constant flow of DVDs coming out (about two new DVDs a month), we're able to hold product hostage, which means we get paid by our retail outlets.

As a self-distributor, you could ship hundreds of copies of your DVD to retailers and then cross your fingers and hope that they decide to honor their commitment to pay you. I can tell you this, you'll be lucky to get paid and in a lot of cases it can take a long time. Your contract may specify that you get paid in thirty or sixty or ninety or 120 days, but in general in the corporate world, invoices are paid at a glacial pace. Whatever the payment commitment is, you can count on the fact that it will take almost twice as long. That is just to be on the safe side. It doesn't mean that all companies break their commitments, but again, the corporate world moves so slowly that you have to count on the fact that you are going to have that long wait period. It's unfortunate, but it's a reality.

TYPICAL DVD DISTRIBUTION DEAL

Your standard DVD distribution deal contains legalese that is best looked at by an attorney. An attorney is an absolute must when closing one of these deals. While you'll want to defer to an attorney who can translate the legalese for you, you will benefit by knowing the key things to look for in a DVD distribution contract. The most important things to you should be:

1. Advance. How much are you going to be paid?
2. Rights. What rights are given up in what territories?
3. Marketing. Defining the marketing obligations of the distributor.
4. Payment timetable. On what kind of schedule do you receive residual payments?
5. Term. The length of the contract.

It helps to understand exactly what an advance is. An advance is money paid on *future* or *anticipated* sales of the film on DVD. So this fee is not a gift, this is money they are advancing you because they *anticipate* that this is something they would pay you out in residuals anyway. They're not just giving it to you up front as a good-will payment.

The reality is that most small DVD distributors do not offer advances. They just don't have the cash reserves of the studios. So you can expect to see a deal that does not include advances. While initially that may seem to be a negative, a zero advance can be used as a negotiating point when it comes to getting things you want that are of a non-monetary value — things such as other rights and control over marketing. Use the point that you will not get an advance to exert further control over the packaging, the marketing plan, the publicity, even the number of DVDs you will receive on a complimentary basis. Always view a negative as negotiating power in your hands.

The next thing to consider is rights. Most domestic DVD distribution deals are for North America, which includes the U.S. and Canada. So be sure that all other territories are open for you to sell the rights. It's also wise for those rights to be spelled out simply in your contract — VHS, DVD, cable television, internet, etc. You may want to reserve the right to sell your DVD through your very own website. If it's important to you, spell it out and be very explicit. (Your lawyer should phrase the wording in accepted contract language.) Take the time to read the contract yourself and while there will be legalese in there, get out a legal dictionary and look up the words you find confusing. Contracts should not be scary or difficult to understand.

Perhaps the most important element in the contract, since it will affect the bottom line and how much money the DVD will eventually make, is how the film will be marketed. Marketing is significant, and these terms are generally not outlined in a contract. You can, however, spell out certain marketing issues in the contract. Marketing issues include things such as mutual approval of the packaging, publicity, etc. No distributor is likely to give the filmmaker total approval of the packaging, but you can ask for mutual approval. Make sure that you know how the film is going to be promoted and any obligation that is possible to spell out in the contract, be sure to ask for those obligations to be spelled out. If the distributor promotes the film well, that will lead to greater sales and better residual payments down the line. It will be difficult to find a DVD distributor that will make all these guarantees, but when you are not receiving an advance, that does give you a certain amount of clout. Don't ever be afraid to ask for something you want; you can spell out anything in a contract.

Also remember that deals are made with people, *not* companies. So carefully evaluate the person you will be dealing with on a regular basis. You may sign a contract with the president of the company, but your account executive will be the one you deal with on every issue, so ask to meet that person. It also helps to do your research. Look at the library of titles that the distributor already has and contact those filmmakers. Do a Google search on a film or filmmaker in their library; it won't be too difficult to track down a filmmaker who has already done a distribution deal with this company. Contact the filmmaker and ask questions like:

"How were you treated?"

"Did the company pay you on time?"

"How well did they sell your movie to consumers?"

Any information you receive should of course be taken with a grain of salt; there will always be bitter filmmakers whose movies didn't sell up to their expectations. It's good to get a wide variety of opinions if possible. But even more important than making money is getting the film promoted and distributed in the right way.

It helps if you look at a distributor that's been successful in a certain genre that is a good match for your film. If this company knows how to sell horror or sci-fi or comedy or animation or whatever, they could be successful with your title as well. Why? Because they have evidence, they have a whole library. Do some more research on this company and find out things like:

— How long have they been in business? If they have been in business less than five years, be cautious.

— Take a look at their library of titles. If they exclusively release sci-fi, fantasy, and horror and they've got 50 titles — what makes you think that they are going to promote your slasher film along with the others? It actually helps to be unique in a certain DVD distributor's library, so that you can be the *only* type of title that they have.

CLOSING THE DEAL — NEGOTIATING YOUR DISTRIBUTION CONTRACT

This small piece of advice works when negotiating any contract. And it's a very simple thing. Find key points in the conversation to remain silent. Do not talk. It sounds easy, but it can be very difficult. This is something I like to do in any negotiation — find a key moment in the flow of the conversation, a place where the other person may be looking for reassurance, and don't say a word. Allow an uncomfortable silence to sit there. The reason for this is that the person you are negotiating with will interpret your silence to mean that something is terribly wrong. The silent treatment is a critical tool in any negotiation, but you need to use it at a certain point in the conversation, generally when you are talking about the parts of the deal that are most important to you.

And you only have to make one distribution deal, so make one that works in your favor.

DELEGATE TASKS EFFECTIVELY

A final word of advice before you begin as the DVD producer of your own movie. You must learn to delegate effectively. For example, if you are not an expert at graphic design, you should certainly not be doing it yourself. Be sure you take a hard look at your skill set. Then look at the skill sets of those around you, and choose the best person for the task. Often, it will not be you. Don't try to do it all. Because when a filmmaker tries to do it all, it becomes evident in a product that is sub-par. I would strongly discourage filmmakers from trying to master every task. In the time it would take you to master certain software or skills, you could have paid someone (or gotten a favor) to do it masterfully.

Moving forward as a filmmaker involves dealing with a lot of failure. It's amazing that some of the most successful have suffered so much failure, but in the face of it they find the strength to move forward. Walt Disney filed for bankruptcy seven times in his career — seven times! Successful people often suffer defeat, but how they deal with it is different than for people who fail. No matter what happens with your DVD, whether you sell one copy or 100,000 copies, if you are determined as a filmmaker you need to continue to move forward in your career.

Section 2

ESSENTIAL ELEMENTS OF A GREAT DVD

These days, a DVD release almost always includes more than just a feature film. You should never consider releasing a "no-frills" DVD, one with limited extras. Plan for your DVD to be a special edition from the git-go. You can always scale back, but consumers now expect discs packed with extra features.

First, it's important to get motivated to make your DVD not just good, but great. Begin by setting up a schedule for yourself. Collect your creative assets so that every aspect of your DVD is the best it can be. You are your own DVD producer. Luckily, the skills you used to make your film are very similar to those required to produce a DVD. You'll just be using those skills in very different ways.

DO IT ONCE, DO IT RIGHT

Let's assume that you don't have a real budget to put together the DVD assets and content that will appear on the disc. I recommend that you use what even the most flat-broke independent filmmaker can take advantage of: *time.* Time is a luxury when you don't have money to spend, so take it. Take your time! Producing your DVD can take as little as six weeks to finish, from compiling the assets to getting the disc authored, approved and pressed. That was the case with *Agent 15*, a Film Threat DVD title. Or it can take as long as nine months, as it did with another Film Threat title, *Frontier.*

I suggest you take the right amount of time for you. For many film-makers, the DVD represents the final version of their movie. Since most people who see the film will see it in the DVD version, you've got to do it right the first time.

Bottom line: You'll only release your DVD once, so take your time and do it right.

DVD TECHNICAL LIMITATIONS

Most of the titles you see on store shelves are DVD-5s, which are *single-layer* DVDs. A DVD-5 disc will hold *up to* 120 minutes of video. Video takes up a lot of space on the disc. Audio, however, does not, so you can have multiple layers of commentary. You could even have two or three commentary tracks if you wish.

A DVD-9 is a *dual-layer* disc which holds up to 240 minutes of video and also costs extra money to press. So while you may consider going over the allotted 120 minutes of video, there will be a cost difference for replication.

Let me spell this out very clearly: A single-layer DVD (DVD-5) will hold 4.4 gigabytes of data, which is *approximately* 120 minutes. The actual running time is not precise and is determined by many factors including bit rates. (Even though a DVD-R holds 4.7 gigabytes, in practical terms it can only fit about 4.45 gigabytes of information; the rest is eaten up by extra information needed to operate the disc.)

Set high standards for your DVD, both for picture quality and for extra features. Even with space limitations, be creative in producing your disc. Use the same level of creative thinking you used to make your film.

Think of this DVD as a showpiece for yourself. Whether you're handing your disc to financiers, agents, studios, or your family, this DVD represents you as a filmmaker. To help you take the next step in your career, make it great. Don't take it so seriously that you end up censoring yourself, but do put your best foot forward on all levels.

Bottom line: Choose whether to produce a DVD-5 or a DVD-9 disc knowing the limitations and be prepared to push those limits.

DVD EXTRA FEATURES — GET CREATIVE

There are only two "extras" on a DVD that are absolutely essential — the *trailer*, since it is also used for marketing, and *commentary*.

The trailer is critical since it will not only be seen on the DVD itself, but should also be streamed on the web as a promotional tool for buyers. The trailer can be anywhere from 30 seconds to two and a half minutes long, but by no means longer than two and a half minutes. A good rule is to keep them wanting more, so a trailer of about a minute or a minute and a half is sufficient. You'll find tips on creating a killer trailer later in this chapter.

The commentary is another feature that DVD viewers have come to expect. The commentary doesn't have to be by the filmmaker (although it often is). Further on in this chapter we'll discuss your commentary options.

There are no rules about the kinds of extras you can put on your DVD. Within reason, at least consider all these possibilities:

- Trailer (A must. More on making a trailer later.)
- Commentary (Another must. And there are all kinds — see section below.)
- Filmmaker's Introduction (See section on **Filmmaker's Intro** below)
- Photo Diary
- Stills Gallery
- Behind-the-Scenes Documentaries and Featurettes
- Foreign-Language subtitles
- Bonus short films (That embarrassing one from early in your career. Or not.)
- Deleted scenes
- Deleted scenes with commentary
- Alternate endings
- Alternate endings with commentary
- Bloopers or outtakes
- Factoid captions/subtitles
- Hidden bonus footage (see section on "Easter Eggs" below)
- Storyboards (with audio or text explanations)
- Festival Q&A (footage shot at a film fest)
- Bios (may include cast bios, key crew and filmmaker bios)
- Music videos (if any were made)
- Marketing materials like posters, promotional photos, etc.
- Link to your official website where additional content may reside
- Credits (a DVD credit section is not required)

There are many more types of extras not included on this list. Make a wish list, then be prepared to be realistic about what is possible to include within your schedule. And don't just think "outside the box" — take a sledgehammer to the box! Smash it and try something totally new that's not even included on the list above. In fact, I would encourage trying something that's *never* been done. For example, the *Swingers* DVD has commentary hosted by writer/actor John Favreau and Vince Vaughan. In addition to the audio commentary track they used a telestrator — basically a device that allows them to draw onto the television image as they're watching it — kind of like a sportscaster giving play-by-play analysis. (Get more info here:

http://www.telestrator.com/) It's very innovative, and with Vince and Fav, very funny too. The two commentators circle parts of the screen and even play games of tic-tac-toe to kill time. It's hilarious and it works for this title. Come up with something new that works for yours.

The only type of extra that I would advise against is any type of game. It requires a mountain of programming and graphics work and generally DVD games tend to be lame. Frankly, games on a DVD are just not worth the trouble.

Don't be afraid to push the limits of the DVD medium. You might consider putting your title up for various DVD awards given out by the numerous organizations that recognize quality and innovation. (Keep in mind that applying for these awards costs money, but it's worthwhile if the result is a trophy that you can use to get attention for your DVD release.)

Bottom line: Make a wish list of the extras you want to appear on your DVD and think creatively with them. A trailer and commentary are the only truly necessary extras, but certainly put as many extra features as possible on the disc. Be forewarned: The more content you include, the more time it will take to assemble those assets.

FILMMAKER'S INTRODUCTION

Let's assume that the average DVD viewer hasn't heard of you or your film. Yes, it's sad, but true. In fact, most of the independent DVD titles littering store shelves are, well, obscure. That's okay. The DVD release is your chance to put your film into a context by providing information about who made the film, and why.

When people see independent films at festivals, the screening is often accompanied by a guest appearance by the filmmaker(s). The experience is often not just about seeing the movie — it's about the person who *made* the movie and what they're all about. Filmmakers at fests will introduce their movie and even engage in a question-and-answer session lasting ten minutes or so. Audiences love seeing films at fests because they have the opportunity to hear directly from the filmmakers in person. Why not include something like this on your own DVD?

A short video offering a "Filmmaker's Introduction" is your opportunity to tell viewers of the DVD *why you made it* and *who you are*. Don't underestimate the power of one of these introductions. It's something like a "director's statement" but produced on video.

Bill Boll designed his DVD *April is My Religion* so that viewers *had* to watch his intro. On *April*, when you press "play," the film begins with Bill's introduction, whether you want to see it or not. In the course of about five minutes Bill introduces himself, tells where he's from, and then goes on to explain what led to the making of his movie, which is based on an unfinished novel. Then his interview segues into a mini-documentary showing stills and behind-the-scenes footage. The production value of this mini-doc is very high as he includes music along with his personal remembrances. Bill's intro adds greatly to the experience of watching *April is My Religion*, creating a personal connection between filmmaker and viewer.

You might include your intro as one of the chapter stops at the beginning of the film. Or have it separate; the choice is yours. The intro can be anywhere from 30 seconds to as long as five minutes or so. (Not too long or audiences will fast forward.) Keep in mind that a filmmaker introduction isn't a commentary: this is you, the filmmaker, looking directly into the camera, explaining to the audience watching the DVD why you made this movie and what you went through to get it done.

Personally, this is my favorite extra feature (next to commentary), and if you only decide to include one custom extra on your disc, this one would be well worth the effort.

Bottom line: A Filmmaker's Introduction can help put your movie into context so audiences will appreciate it even more.

RECORDING COMMENTARY

A good commentary track is perhaps the most important element in making a successful DVD. A killer commentary track for a crappy film can actually result in a positive review for your DVD from critics. And a lousy commentary can also have an impact, resulting in a negative DVD review for an otherwise solid movie.

Personally, I am addicted to DVD commentaries. In fact, I listen to them daily as I work, kind of like talk radio. *I absolutely love them!* I can easily tell you what makes a *good* one and what makes a *bad* one. What you may be surprised to learn is that an outstanding filmmaker is not always capable of telling compelling stories on a DVD commentary track. Sometime it's the opposite, and you can hear some truly wonderful commentary tracks recorded by cinema's worst hacks.

Filmmakers Who Give Good Commentary

An example of a filmmaker who consistently records excellent commentary is Steven Soderbergh, director of *sex, lies, and videotape, Ocean's Eleven* (and *Twelve*), *Traffic, Erin Brokovich,* and so on. Soderbergh always hosts his commentary with the screenwriters of his films and introduces the commentary track by saying "*Hey, welcome to another episode of two white guys talking about movies...*"

What makes Soderbergh's commentary so effective is that he hits on almost every aspect of what you'd look for in a good commentary.

First of all, he offers *insight into his process.* We learn firsthand how he makes movies and his philosophies on cinema. Soderbergh will explain why he did what he did and — he's his own worst critic — he'll even tell you whether he thought it worked or not.

Secondly, we *get to know about him as a person.* Despite all his success, he's a strangely humble and regular guy. He reveals personal history, elements of his family life as they relate to the film, where he went to school, where he came from, who influenced him, favorite films, where he stole ideas, etc. Soderbergh also displays a great sense of humor.

Finally, Soderbergh's commentaries always include lots of *inside stories and anecdotes* about the actors, the financing, the problems, the marketing, the studio, etc. He's not afraid to appear vulnerable or even get into an argument with the screenwriters co-hosting the commentary on the disc. Listen to the commentary track for *The Limey* and you'll hear Soderbergh's heated argument with the screenwriter over cut scenes. It's brilliant!

Other filmmakers who excel at commentary are actor Bruce Campbell — he's hysterical — just listen to any of his commentaries for the *Evil Dead* movies. (By contrast, director Sam Raimi's commentary for *Evil Dead* is terrible. He's very withdrawn and offers no insight or anything personal. In fact, Sam doesn't even talk much.) On Darren Aronofsky's commentary for *Requiem for a Dream* you'll learn about the guerilla style in which that film was made. It's fascinating info. Filmmaker and B-movie legend Lloyd Kaufman's words on the *Citizen Toxie* DVD are simply *pee-your-pants funny* — his tongue is firmly planted in cheek as he flat out lies to play with the viewer and he does it all completely dead pan.

Filmmakers Who Give Bad Commentary

There are many others that offer examples of *bad* commentary. Listen, for example, to Tim Burton on the commentary for *Edward Scissorhands*. He's just not very talkative and he even has trouble articulating complete thoughts. Sometimes these filmmakers aren't particularly good communicators when it comes to explaining their creative process with their audience.

Make a Commentary Outline

You should begin your commentary by introducing yourself and any others that are going to host the commentary with you. You may want to include some subtitles when people talk if the voices are not clearly distinct.

Make sure you plan your commentary with an outline, so there will be no lapses in the conversation. Dead air is just dead. Have an outline as a crutch, but don't think you must rigidly adhere to it. Break your outline into different categories:

- Personal stories and reflections
- Anecdotes about all aspects of the production
- Insight into your filmmaking process

Questions you might ask yourself or address:

- Why did I make this film?
- What led to making this film?
- How long did it take to shoot?
- How much did it cost to make this movie? (You don't have to be specific on the dollar amounts.)

- How did you get financing together?
- What were some of your production struggles?
- What are your influences?

The More, Sometimes Not the Merrier

Of course it's important to have good audio, so use lapel microphones pinned to your collar and do not forget to do an audio test. DVDs that have badly recorded sound will result in users hitting the eject button, or worse, critics offering negative reviews. If you choose to include other people on the commentary track, balance the conversation and act as a host. As the film-maker, you have to run it. If you do not feel comfortable in the "host" role, get a critic or someone else to do it. Make sure the additional people are there for a reason. If you have multiple people in the room during the commentary, you should conduct yourselves like you would if you were on radio — *only one person should speak at a time.*

Environment is Key

It's very important to record your commentary in a *personal* environment. The reason so many major studio movie commentaries are bland is that they are recorded in a lavishly expensive recording studio, with the participants sitting on black leather sofas complete with a mini-fridge filled with bottled water and Diet Cokes. You know, a very sterile environment. You can't expect anyone to get too personal boxed up in a place that feels like a doctor's office.

Choose a very *personal* environment in which to record your commentary. The audio quality may not be the absolute best, but as long as you are miked correctly, the audio will be fine. Content is key here. The environment you choose could be your own home or apartment, at your desk where you edited the movie, at a bar, in one of the key locations for the film, in your favorite movie theater or video store, at the production studio where you made the movie, your basement, your old apartment, just a place that *means* something. Make it personal. And when you begin, *make reference to where you are and its significance.*

When you record your own commentary, please don't sit there and pat yourself on the back. You'll just alienate your audience with tales of "how great that shot is." Let the audience decide whether it was a great shot or not. It's better to be humble than boastful.

Keep Recording

No matter what happens, keep recording. If something goes wrong while you are taping, keep recording. If your mom calls during the middle of the session, pick up the phone, answer it, say, "*Mom, I'm recording the commentary for my movie and I'll have to call you back,*" then keep that in the final audio.

If you spill a drink during the recording session, clean it up and keep going. If anything bad happens (within reason), just keep recording. It's okay to make mistakes. In fact, if the recording is less than perfect, *that's cool!* Minor flaws will be endearing to the listener because, let's face it, that's exactly what you would expect from a *true* independent film.

For example, on the Film Threat DVD *Starwoids*, a documentary about all the fans who waited in line to see *Star Wars Episode I*, director Dennis Przywara recorded his commentary three times in order to get it right. The third time it was much better because he recorded it at one of his subject's apartment. Things went south when someone in the apartment above started playing their guitar really loud. While we couldn't hear the noise on the commentary (they were miked well), it was funny to hear Dennis' reaction to the music as they tried to get the guy to stop playing so they could finish the commentary. Mistakes like this are personal and human and make for interesting commentaries.

CREATIVE COMMENTARY

Consider getting creative with your commentary tracks. For example, Film Threat DVD's *Jar Jar Binks: The F! True Hollywood Story* contains a "fake" George Lucas commentary with a Lucas sound-alike making comments about *Star Wars*.

I recorded three commentary tracks for my own short film *Red*. The first commentary had the usual things you would expect from a commentary, which included myself and the cinematographer, David E. Williams. The second commentary was recorded after Dave and I drank a six pack of beer. It's identified on the disc as our "Drunk Commentary." So users have a choice to listen to the regular commentary or a "Drunk Commentary" where Dave and I slur through embarrassing stories. The third commentary track was from one of the production assistants on the film, Justin Stanley. He is now an established and successful screenwriter, but at the time, he was my lackey. (No offense, Justin; you were a good one.)

Roger Avary's DVD for *The Rules of Attraction* includes five different commentaries! One is, of course, director Avary himself talking about the film; one includes key crew members like the production designer, cinematographer, etc.; and another includes what is identified on the disc as the "Revolving" commentary. Since the film has an ensemble cast, this commentary was executed so that when a particular actor's scene comes up, that actor begins to comment. When that actor's scene is over, another actor takes up where that person left off. Avary also included a commentary by redhaired comedian Carrot Top. No, I'm not kidding. Go rent the disc if you don't believe me. Avary wanted to include a commentary track from someone who had never seen the movie before. Carrot Top is freaked out by the flick and his on-the-fly remarks are actually entertaining. So when it comes to commentary, keep in mind that you can do anything. *Anything!* So get creative!

The Film Threat DVD release of the film *Jerkbeast* included a commentary track by famous underground cartoonists such as Coop, Johnny Ryan, Tim Maloney, and Tony Millionaire. This roundtable of cartoonists ripped on the film with the worst imaginable insults. It makes for an extremely entertaining commentary track, even though we learn virtually nothing about the film itself.

You could invite a critic to comment on your movie — heck, even a critic who hated the movie. You might want to get a comedian, an actor, someone not affiliated with the film, someone famous, someone who is a big supporter of the film, just someone that would add an interesting element to a commentary track. Have some guts and consider having the PA that got the brunt of everyone's abuse during the making of the film do a commentary track, that might be funny.

Recording a commentary doesn't necessarily mean that you will use it. If it turns out poorly, just don't use it. Keep in mind that when others are involved, you need to produce these commentaries as you would your own, so make sure the subject(s) stay focused on the task at hand. Other people included in the commentary should be just as prepared as you are with notes, stories, etc.

Here are the types of commentary you might consider:
- Director commentary
- Filmmaker commentary (include the cinematographer, producer, key personnel, etc.)
- Cast commentary (key cast members and actors)
- Crew commentary (key production staff)
- Cinematographer commentary
- Special effects commentary
- PA commentary
- Screenwriter commentary
- Commentary hosted by a film historian, critic, other filmmaker or film luminary that will help sell the DVD
- Director's Mom's commentary
- Commentary by someone prominent who has never seen the film
- Critic commentary
- Naked truth commentary (do the commentary in the nude, or clothed, no one has to know)
- Stoned commentary (would have been good for *Dazed & Confused*)
- Drunk commentary

Don't Forget to Introduce Yourself At the Start

Begin your commentary by introducing yourself, perhaps offer some personal words about your beginnings as a filmmaker and then launch right into it. In the end, the viewer should learn something about filmmaking, get insight into you as a filmmaker, all the while being entertained as they listen.

Bottom line: Commentary is critical. A successful commentary includes insight into the filmmaking process, anecdotes about the movie, and a chance to get to know you as a person and filmmaker. Also consider producing additional commentary tracks from others involved in the production as well as noteworthy film figures. You may also want to think about a clever way to approach the commentary such as a unique location, co-hosting it with a famous film figure, or even doing your commentary in an altered state.

TRAILER DOS AND DON'TS

A trailer should be considered a "must" feature for a DVD. The only rule — make the trailer no longer than two and a half minutes — that's 150 seconds and shorter is generally preferred. Here's what you should know:

Ten Elements of an Explosively Effective Trailer

1. Quick Cuts. If you've got some cool shots and a really simple-minded story, cut each shot down to about a 1/3 of a second and slap on some pumping driving music. The unfortunate reality is that often style wins over substance.

2. Use Graphics That Grab You. Decent graphics are a plus. Be creative and make a title treatment with impact that is different from your main title.

3. Original Music is Important. Be careful of what music you use. There are plenty of affordable tracks by companies that supply music specifically for trailers. Be sure to use music that is legally cleared. Otherwise, there's another way. *Music Industry Dirty Little Secret:* For the purposes of the trailer only, if you want music that sounds like a certain movie soundtrack in order to capture a particular mood, have an original song or piece of music composed. The secret is, if you want to blatantly rip off a tune, remember to change every seventh note. By changing the tune slightly, you will avoid being sued.

4. Tell the Story (But Don't Ruin It.) If you've got a great story, don't be afraid to spell it out. It doesn't hurt to do a little handholding. A narrator can go a long way toward dramatizing the story in broad strokes. But don't tell the whole story. Leave them wanting more.

5. Use Positive Reviews. If the film has gotten early positive reviews from notable critics or credible press outlets, use them. Big, bold quotes in a white typeface against a black background look impressive cut quickly into the trailer. Generally, these are most effectively used near the end, just before the title screen. Be sure to clear the use of these quotes from the outlets that provided them.

6. Great Sound is Critical. Spend time on the sound mix. If you have a slight problem understanding what the actor said, then you can bet your ass that the guy looking at your trailer doesn't have a clue as to what was spoken. Also, don't be afraid to record dialog for the trailer only in order to clarify the story.

7. Star Power. If your film has a recognizable star, make sure to feature your star very prominently. Even if you've got only one celebrity in a cameo, make sure those shots are used extensively in the trailer.

8. Keep it Short. The shorter the better, about a minute or two, but absolutely make sure it is under two and a half minutes. Why? Because that is the time limit imposed by the MPAA for all theatrical trailers. The audience watching your little masterpiece have been trained like a kennel full of Pavlov's dogs. Anything over two and a half minutes and they're looking at their watches.

9. Start with a Bang! Open with an attention grabber. Opening with an explosive image or a memorable line of dialog will keep them watching.

10. End with a Bang! Close with the best shot and/or best line.

Ten Trailer "Don'ts"

1. Don't Use a Feature Editor. Use a trailer editor, if possible, and don't even consider hiring your feature editor to cut the trailer. A feature editor is used to letting things play out and is not as good at the short sell. A trailer is an advertisement, plain and simple. It's essentially a commercial or a music video and is a completely different animal than a feature, so get a good editor with experience cutting trailers.

2. Don't Fear Outtakes. Don't be afraid to use some original scenes or outtakes that didn't make the final cut. Remember in *Twister* when that tractor came crashing down in front of that car? Nope, me neither... it existed only in the trailer. It's also fine to shoot footage specifically for the trailer.

3. No Nudity. Keep the trailer PG-13 at least. Even if your film has a lot of sex, there's no reason to flaunt it. Violence, of course, is never frowned upon. But you never know who may see it or download it. Make sure the trailer is acceptable to air on network television.

4. No Expanded Scenes. Use sound bites only. Don't use really long expository dialog. Make every shot concise.

5. Boring is Bad. Get to the point. What's your movie about? Define it in the first ten seconds.

6. Do Not Use Uncleared Music. You'll be shooting yourself in the foot by using music for which you don't have the rights.

7. Bad Transfer. Make sure not to skimp on the transfer. The picture should look as good or even better than your feature. Footage from your dailies or rough cut is not suitable for use. Be sure to transfer clean for the trailer.

8. Never Use Stolen Shots. Eventually, they'll see the finished film, so don't try to cut in expensive shots that are gratuitously lifted from another movie like a giant explosion.

9. Do Not Give Away the Ending. Never, ever give away the ending. Yeah, I know that trailers for big studio movies do it all the time, but you still shouldn't do it.

10. Not Too Long. The most common crime committed by an amateur trailer editor is cutting one that is too long. Shorter is better.

Bottom line: Trailers are a must-have feature and their purpose is to sell the movie. Period.

DVD EASTER EGGS — HIDDEN SECRETS

"Easter eggs" are hidden extras included on the DVD that are not listed as one of the special features. Film freaks and collectors love Easter eggs as they are like the *free* prize inside a box of cereal. For example, *April is my Religion* contains an extra scene — a hidden outtake of a nude scene. *Jar Jar Binks: The F! True Hollywood Story* has Easter eggs hidden on each of its menu screens — simply highlight the graphic of Jar Jar using the remote and click "play" for a bonus scene not listed on the disc. It's an opportunity to include more content for the true film geeks. Even better, it also creates another opportunity for publicity, because you can tell people to come to your website to find all of your Easter eggs.

Come up with a simple way for users to find the Easter egg such as highlighting a graphic using the remote. Generally these hidden features lead users to a strange piece of video or a text screen with a special message. *Whatever you do, have fun with this!*

Bottom line: Easter Eggs are not absolutely necessary, but they are a great way for fans to "discover" additional content on your disc.

TEXT-BASED EXTRA FEATURES

While video takes up the bulk of the data on the disc, and audio takes up much less, text takes up virtually no space. So consider using text-based data or additional screens to add to the experiences on the disc. Each of your deleted scenes might include a very short paragraph of text explaining why the scene was cut, what the scene is, where it would have been in the film, what led to the decision of cutting it, etc.

You could include text-based features like a filmmaker's diary, production notes, or a list of credits and bios for each person involved with your film. Film Threat's DVD *Agent 15* has a "Credits" section in which each person's bio is seen when their name is highlighted.

Caution: The average television set in the U.S. is 19-inch diagonal, so be sure any text-based features are readable on a smaller TV. Generally white text against a black background works well, but always keep optimum readability in mind — and you can include multiple screens for your text-based features.

Bottom line: Consider text content as a way to expand your extras. Text also does not take up much space on the disc.

BONUS EXTRAS ON YOUR OFFICIAL WEBSITE

If you have extra content that doesn't fit onto your DVD, consider putting the best deleted scenes/diary material/full script, etc. onto a secret area of your film's web site. Create a hidden area on your website for extras that won't fit on the disk and make them available to purchasers of your title. It's also a great way to interact with buyers of your DVD as some may choose to e-mail you after viewing the film.

Consider making the link a hidden part of your site, so that only owners of the DVD can find it — like *www.yourmovietitle.com/dvdextras.*

Bottom line: If you are having trouble fitting all your extras onto your DVD, include a link to your web site where bonus material may reside.

Section 3 PREPARING YOUR DVD ASSETS

DVD PROJECT: GETTING STARTED

In this section you will learn how to make a DVD from scratch. Using a fictitious DVD project as a model, you will be guided through the steps needed to author your own DVD project.

- ▸ STEP 1: DETERMINING YOUR ASSETS

- ▸ STEP 2: FLOWCHART

- ▸ STEP 3: BIT BUDGET

- ▸ STEP 4: PREPARATION OF VIDEO

- ▸ STEP 5: PREPARATION OF AUDIO

- ▸ STEP 6: PREPARATION OF MENUS

- ▸ STEP 7: PREPARATION OF STILLS AND SLIDESHOWS

- ▸ STEP 8: SUBTITLES

This basic sequence can be applied to any DVD project. Let's get started!

▸ STEP 1: DETERMINING YOUR ASSETS

When venturing into unknown territory, it's smart to have a map in hand before setting off on an adventure. The same goes for setting up your DVD.

In Section II we discussed the possible "extras" that might appear on your DVD. So the first step, and the easiest, is to define your content. How much do you have? Are we talking just a movie and a trailer or are we talking a movie, a trailer, a behind-the-scenes documentary, still galleries, cast and crew bios, and more? These are your "assets," and once they are determined, you can move on to the structure of your DVD.

I've decided to make a DVD for a (non-existent) movie called *Stranded*.

While traveling cross-country, a couple finds their relationship at a breaking point. After an argument at a rest stop, the man drives off, leaving the woman in the middle of nowhere with nothing but the clothes on her back. Through a series of adventures as she makes her way home, she learns to know herself better and gains insight into the problems in their relationship.

Let's say that other than the movie itself, I have a behind-the-scenes documentary, some pictures that were taken during the shoot, and a great trailer. I also want to include bios of the director, the writer, and two of the actors, plus a commentary by the director. That's already a good amount of "value-added content."

Value-Added Content — This concept is what drives ever-increasing DVD sales. The idea is that the DVD experience should transcend just the viewing of the movie. The content is typically referred to as "Special Features" or "Extras." The first major special feature was the audio commentary. Since then, DVD producers have been upping the ante to the point where you can now get a four-disc set devoted to one movie such as *The Lord of the Rings: The Return of The King Collector's Edition.* This set is packed with over ten hours of extras that literally dissect the creation of the film in its entirety.

Keep in mind that most of this content was planned for ahead of time and set into motion during the actual production of the film. In other words, if you want an extensive "making of" documentary, you need to have the footage shot while you are making the movie.

Value-Added Content has become so important that productions are preparing for it before they have even rolled a single frame of film.

At this point you should make a list of all the assets that you want on your DVD based on what you have available and/or what you want to create.

Below is a list of common assets:

VIDEO OPTIONS

Main Feature
Behind-the-Scenes Featurette
Cast & Crew Interviews
Director's Introduction
Deleted Scenes
Stills (Picture) Gallery
Extended Scenes
Trailer

Trailers (other than Main Movie)

Radio Spots

Gag Reel

Music Video

Outtakes

Storyboard to Film Comparison

Short Film

AUDIO OPTIONS

2.0 Dolby Digital Stereo Sound

5.1 Dolby Digital Stereo Sound

6.1 DTS Surround Sound

Audio Commentary Track

2nd Audio Commentary Track

3rd Audio Commentary Track

TEXT OPTIONS

Cast & Crew Bios

Movie Website Information

Production Notes

Text on Screen (other)

Trivia Test

DVD Credits

For *Stranded*, I've decided on these assets.

▸ Main Feature

▸ Trailer

▸ Behind-the-Scenes Featurette

▸ Cast & Crew Bios

▸ Stills (Picture) Gallery

▸ Director's Commentary

▸ STEP 2: FLOWCHART

Now that we have a general idea of what will be included on the *Stranded* DVD, the next step is to construct a basic flowchart. The flowchart is a valuable companion during the authoring stage. (The authoring process will be covered in the next section.) This is the map that we spoke of earlier. It gives you a graphical representation of your DVD project that can be used to organize and keep track of your assets so that nothing wilil be left out or forgotten. I can't stress enough how this simple step will make your life much easier.

Creating this hierarchy is a way to organize your assets: which are the most important to access and which are the least. There are no set rules about what kind of assets are more important; it's more a matter of personal preference and common sense. On the other hand, having your "Play Main Feature" button on a sub-menu is probably not the best idea. Don't lose sight of the fact that, despite all the attractive extras, the number one reason people are buying the DVD is for the movie itself.

BEFORE YOU START: SUB-MENUS ADD VALUE AND AID NAVIGATION

In theory, all of your content could be organized onto one main menu. For a DVD containing only a few assets, this makes sense. As you add more extra features, however, you'll want to consider using sub-menus to help organize the assets and to give the viewer easier access to them.

There are several sub-menus that you may want to consider using as you map out your DVD. These sub-menus are not dictated by the assets; in other words, you could live without them. Having multiple menus, including sub-menus, expands the graphical interface of your DVD and makes consumers feel like they are really getting their money's worth.

SCENE SELECTION MENU

Let's start with the "Scene Selection" sub-menu. This is a menu (or series of menus) that allows the viewer to start at a determined point in the movie. It's the equivalent of chapters in a book, so that's why it's also sometimes called "Chapter Selection." You will need to predetermine these place cards yourself (see next chapter), and the selectable scenes are the buttons that jump you to a specific point within the track.

These "chapters" are usually numbered and/or named. Naming can be a challenge. The best advice is to refer to the first line of dialogue of the particular chapter (e.g. "A bigger boat") or an overall thematic or plot description (e.g. Surprise attack! or The shark strikes). Try not to over-intellectualize the task. Keep it simple yet descriptive: using four words or less makes it a lot easier when it comes time to design the menus. And if all else fails, there is always "Chapter One," "Chapter Two," etc.

Don't go crazy with chapters. The average 90-minute movie has 12-15 chapters.

SET-UP MENU

Many DVDs have a Set-Up menu to allow the viewer to choose how they are going to view the film. A typical DVD may contain a 2.0 Stereo version of the movie's audio as well as a 5.1 Dolby Digital and/or DTS audio track. The viewer obviously needs to decide which audio track they want to listen to. There is usually a default audio (2.0 Stereo is the norm). This menu might also include the subtitle selections, which may be as simple as English Subtitles "On" or "Off" or as complex as four (or more) languages to choose from.

Some DVD Producers include the Director's Commentary in the Set-up Menu. For our DVD project it is in the Special Features Menu. If you have both a Set-Up Menu and a Special Features Menu and choose to access the Commentary by way of the Special Features Menu, be aware that this could lead to some confusion, by making it seem possible to choose the Director's Commentary in the Special Features Menu and still be able to choose 5.1 Dolby Digital in the Set-Up Menu. One way to avoid the confusion is to simply have the feature begin immediately when you activate the Commentary button in the Special Features menu.

DVD CREDITS MENU

As DVD production and authoring became an integral, and respected, part of the DVD process, it became clear that the individuals involved would want credit for their contributions. Especially as the quality of menu design and extras may at times rival the main feature. Thus was born the DVD credits page. Usually this button takes the form of a company logo or a specialized shape that sets it apart from the "normal" selections.

EASTER EGGS

As mentioned in Section II, an "Easter egg" is a hidden track, slideshow, or menu on a DVD that, depending on how sly the DVD author chooses to be, is moderately tough to downright impossible to find.

The button might be a picture or some text that at first glance appears to be part of the background. If however you happened to hit the left arrow button on your controller while you were on the set-up button, the hidden track would become selected. My advice on Easter eggs is to use them sparingly. It's always fun for the consumer to find something unexpected on a DVD, but if they spend more time hunting for the damn button than watching your content, you've kind of defeated the purpose. Frustrating the consumer is usually not the best way to experience a product or a way to inspire purchasing recommendations.

An example of an Easter egg might be a short film that the director made in college. This is a fun idea for a DVD project because, even though it doesn't have direct relevance to the main material, it does offer something that a dedicated viewer might appreciate seeing.

Other popular Easter eggs are blooper reels, outtakes, trailers, promotional materials, or even an alternative version of the main feature. You are limited only by your creativity (and space on the disc, of course).

Let's get back to the creation of the flowchart. I have decided that I want to add some of these sub-menus to organize my DVD assets better.

Once again my assets for this DVD are:

▸ Main Feature
▸ Trailer
▸ Behind-the-Scenes Featurette
▸ Cast & Crew Bios
▸ Still (Picture) Gallery
▸ Director's Commentary

My Menus will be as follows:
- Main Menu
- Scene Selection Sub-Menu
- Special Features Sub-Menu

Now that we have the basis of our *Stranded* DVD we are ready to begin. So grab a piece of paper and a pencil and follow my lead.

There are programs such as VISID and Inspiration that create flowcharts but I've found a simple sheet of paper (turned lengthwise) and three different highlighter colors (to mark which boxes are Tracks, Menus or Slideshows) do the trick.

MAKING THE FLOWCHART

Start by drawing a box at the top and labeling it "Main Menu." The Main Menu will typically access the Main Feature, Scene Selection, and Special Features. It may also link to a Set-Up menu and/or DVD Credits menu if you so desire.

The Main Menu will contain these three options:
- Play Feature
- Scene Selection
- Special Features

Next draw a box for each of the three options below the Main Menu box and label them "TRACK: *Stranded* Feature," "SCENE SELECTION MENU," and "SPECIAL FEATURES MENU." I suggest making the Scene Selection and Special Features sub-menu boxes a bit larger to accommodate the option text.

The Scene Selection Menu will contain these six options:
- Chapter 1: Vacation
- Chapter 2: Dumped
- Chapter 3: Hitchin'
- Chapter 4: Despair
- Chapter 5: Realization
- Chapter 6: Homecoming

The Special Features Menu will contain these five options:

▸ Behind-the-Scenes Featurette

▸ Trailer

▸ Director's Commentary

▸ Cast & Crew Bios

▸ Stills Gallery

With a line, connect the Main Menu box to each of the sub-boxes (i.e. three separate lines).

You will now draw four more boxes beneath the Special Features menu, one for each of its options. Label them "TRACK: Behind-the-Scenes Featurette," "TRACK: Trailer," "Stills Gallery," and "Cast & Crew Bios Menu." As with the Special Features Menu, make the Cast & Crew Bios sub-menu box large enough to accommodate the text.

The Cast & Crew Bios Menu will contain these four options:

▸ Writer/Director's Bio

▸ Producer's Bio

▸ Actor #1 Bio

▸ Actor #2 Bio

With a line, connect the Special Features Menu box to each of the new boxes (i.e. four separate lines).

Finally, draw four boxes beneath the Cast & Crew Bios menu. Label them "Writer/ Director's Bio Menu," "Producer's Bio Menu," "Actor #1 Bio Menu" and "Actor #2 Bio Menu."

With a line, connect the Cast & Crew Bios menu box to each of the new boxes (i.e. four separate lines).

Use three different highlighter markers. Choose one color to represent Menus, one to represent Tracks, and the third for the Stills Gallery.

When you are done it should look something like this. *(See diagram on the following page).*

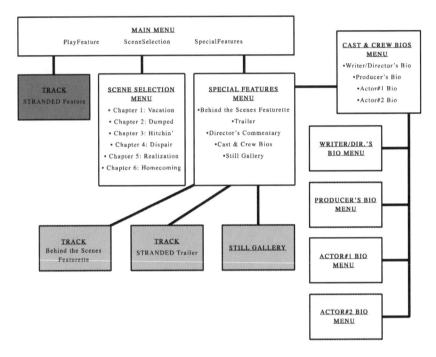

Now that you have the flowchart laid out before you, it is easy to see all the assets you will ultimately need to create the DVD. I suggest breaking it down by tracks, menus, and slideshows. This is the terminology used by DVD Studio Pro and it will avoid confusion when we get to the authoring section.

The *Stranded* DVD Assets:

Tracks

‣ Movie (with 5.1 AC-3 Dolby Digital Surround)
‣ Behind-the-Scenes Featurette (with 2.0 AC-3 Dolby Digital Stereo)
‣ Trailer (with 2.0 AC-3 Dolby Digital Stereo)

Menus

‣ Main Menu (Motion Menu with 16-Bit Stereo PCM 48kHz)*
‣ Scene Selection Menu
‣ Special Features Menu
‣ Cast & Crew Bios Menu
‣ Writer/Director's Bio Menu
‣ Producer's Bio Menu

▸ Actor #1 Bio Menu

▸ Actor #2 Bio Menu

Slideshows

▸ Stills Gallery

Your first question may be why I've lumped the individual Cast & Crew Bios with the menus. The reason is because any page with a button is a menu (after you've read the information from the bio page you need to be able to get back to the previous menu, which requires a button).

One way around this is by making the individual bios a series of images in a slideshow. This method is completely acceptable, but for our purposes I want them to have navigational buttons.

You will also notice that I've decided that my Main Menu will be a Motion Menu. You want to decide which menus will be Motion or Static at this point because Motion Menus require a lot more space than static ones and this is necessary to know when heading into Step 3. (Motion and Static Menus are explained in more detail in Step 6.)

ORGANIZATION

Before you dive headlong into your computer, it's best to have some folders set up beforehand. There are a great number of assets that you will need to keep track of, beyond the ones necessary for the actual authoring of the DVD. Keeping these in a logical hierarchy will make the project go much more smoothly and keep you from wasting time trying to hunt down a mis-

placed file. The first thing to do is create a folder on your desktop and name it with the title of your DVD. In our case we will call it (that's right) STRANDED DVD.

Next you want to set up some folders within the STRANDED DVD Folder. These will apply to virtually all DVDs.

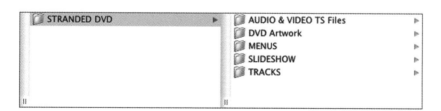

AUDIO & VIDEO TS FILES

This folder will remain empty until you are ready to build the finished DVD project. You will be asked where to place these most important files in the muxing process. Setting it up at this point will save you a step later.

DVD ARTWORK

This is a place to store all the graphics associated with the packaging of the finished DVD. If you are planning to just burn the discs at home on blank DVD-Rs and stick them in a paper sleeve, then this folder may have no relevance to you. But if you're planning to have them professionally replicated with disc and box art (a.k.a. case wraps), then you'll want to keep those files stored with the rest. Typically I'll set up sub-folders before I need them in the DVD Artwork folder.

Create one folder for the case wraps, one for the disc art and another for the insert artwork (if your project requires one). Because you will probably have multiple variations of each, this is a better method of keeping track of them.

MENUS

The Menus folder will contain all the different menus you'll need to create for the DVD project. If any of your menus are Motion Menus, I recommend creating sub-folders to contain all the necessary files for each Motion Menu.

Because our Main Menu has video, sound, and button highlight overlays, create a sub-folder called Main Menu in which to store all those files. We will also need a sub-folder to hold the four Cast & Crew Bio menus that we will be making.

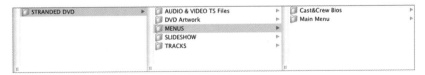

SLIDESHOW

This folder will ultimately contain all the graphics that you have created for your projects. If you have multiple slideshows, then I would suggest creating sub-folders for each within the Slideshow folder (for example, Stills Gallery, Cast & Crew, Production Notes, etc.).

TRACKS

Finally, the Tracks folder will contain all the video, audio, and subtitles for each individual track within your project. Because we already know what we want on the Stranded DVD, we can go ahead and make sub-folders for each of them: Behind the Scenes, Main Feature, Trailer.

Each of these folders will eventually contain an MPEG-2 (.m2v) file and at least one audio file. If you have multiple audio or subtitle files for an individual video file, they should be stored within the same sub-folder.

I know this seems like a lot of set-up to do before you even start, but every little bit helps. You will find that there can be an overwhelming number of necessary files. Having them filed away in logical places will save you a lot of headaches later on.

Another reason why this kind of organizational hierarchy is so important is that if someone other than you is going to author the DVD they will have an intuitive way of finding the files they need.

▸ STEP 3: BIT BUDGET

I've decided what I want on the *Stranded* DVD. Now I've got to figure out how much space I'm going to need.

First, you should get to know your options, as there are many different types of DVD media (*see chart on the following page*).

A common misconception is that a DVD-5 can hold two hours (120 minutes) of footage, period. This is a highly inaccurate way of determining disc space because there are so many factors that account for how much actual footage you can fit on the DVD. The space capacity is based on megabits of information, not time.

DISC CAPACITY CHART			
DISC NAME	DISC TYPE	DISC CAPACITY	REAL DATA CAPACITY
DVD-5	Single-sided/Single-layer	4.7 GB	4.38 GB
DVD-9	Single-sided/Dual-layer	8.54 GB	7.92 GB
DVD-10	Dual-sided/Single-layer	9.4 GB	8.75 GB
DVD-18	Dual-sided/Dual-layer	17.08 GB	15.8 GB

However, you can use two hours as a rough estimate for a little common-sense preplanning. Say you have a movie that is 110 minutes long and you have two featurettes, each of which is 15 minutes long. Simple math will tell you that you already have two hours and 20 minutes of footage (not including the menus or any other features you may want to add). It's obvious that it won't fit on a DVD-5, so you must either remove assets from the DVD or step up to a DVD-9 or DVD-10.

If you are planning on burning your DVDs on your home computer than you are limited to DVD-5 discs. Any other disc types must be manufactured at a replication facility and you will have to provide them with a DLT (Digital Linear Tape) or a DVD-R Master.

Fortunately there is a way of figuring out how much space your particular project will need. The process of calculating this is known as your Bit Budget.

Doing a Bit Budget will also help you determine what average "Bit Rate" you will need to encode your video assets. (More on that in Step 4: Preparation of Video.) Choosing a reasonable bit rate is another way of maximizing the capacity of the DVD media you have chosen for your project.

Bit Rate — You'll need to understand this important term. It refers to the number of bits per second that make up video and audio assets. The rates range from 1 to 9.8 Mbps (megabits per second). The higher the bit rate, the better the quality of the image. This is based on what appears in any given second of video. For instance, a cluttered scene with a lot of movement would need a higher bit rate in order to display the image cleanly, while on the other hand, a static image with not much going on would only need a low bit rate to look good. It's important to realize, though, that a higher bit rate will mean a larger file size, thus less useable space on the DVD.

The maximum bit rate that a DVD player can read is 10.08 Mbps, but using a bit rate higher than 8 Mbps is not recommended. Most people's instinct is to go for the highest they can get, but there is a problem in the fact that the bit rate works in tandem with the video's audio and subtitle files. The more layers of audio or subtitles you have add to the overall bit rate. So even encoding the video at a rate of 8 Mbps can be risky if you have, say, two audio layers and a commentary track as well as subtitles. Having too high a bit rate can not only affect the ability of your DVD player to play the disc, but it might also crash your DVD file while muxing the project (more on that later).

Most mainstream movies that you buy at the store use an average bit rate of 5 to 5.5 Mbps. They do this in order to save space so they can cram as much stuff on the discs as possible. But they are using top-of-the-line, hardware-based encoders that give them the highest quality even at these low bit rates.

Getting back to our *Stranded* DVD, let's look at the running time of our video assets. We need to know how many seconds of video footage we have. (The Motion menu is a video file, so it must be included in our calculations.)

Main Feature = 94 min. (x 60 sec.) = 5,640 seconds
Trailer = 2 min. (x 60 sec.) = 120 seconds
Behind-the-Scenes Featurette = 7 min. (x 60 sec.) = 420 seconds
Main Menu = 1 min. (x 60 sec.) = 60 seconds
Total = 104 min. (x 60 sec.) = 6,240 seconds

Next we need to determine how much space the audio will take up. The chart on the following page shows the bit rates for the most common audio formats.

AUDIO BIT RATE CHART

AUDIO FORMAT	BIT RATE
AC-3 2.0 Stereo	.192 Mbps
AC-3 5.1 Surround	.448 Mbps
16-Bit Stereo PCM (48kHz)	1.536 Mbps
24-Bit Stereo PCM (96kHz)	4.608 Mbps

By multiplying the length of each track (in seconds) by the bit rate we can determine the amount of space (in Mbits) each audio file requires.

Main Feature (5.1 AC-3) = 5,640 sec. x .448 Mbps = 2,527 Mbits

Director's Commentary (2.0 AC-3) = 5,640 sec. x .192 Mbps = 1,083 Mbits

Trailer (2.0 AC-3) = 120 sec. x .192 Mbps = 23 Mbits

Behind the Scenes Featurette (2.0 AC-3) = 420 sec. x .192 Mbps = 81 Mbits

Main Menu (16-Bit/48kHz) = 60 sec. x 1.536 Mbps = 93 Mbits

Total Audio = 3,807 Mbits

We need one more piece of information in order to finish up our Bit Budget. The following chart shows the actual storage capacity of each type of DVD media.

TOTAL DISC CAPACITY CHART

DISC NAME	BIT CAPACITY	-5% RESERVE	TOTAL BIT CAPACITY
DVD-5	37,600 Mbits	1,880 Mbits	35,720 Mbits
DVD-9	68,320 Mbits	3,416 Mbits	64,904 Mbits
DVD-10	75,200 Mbits	3,760 Mbits	71,440 Mbits
DVD-18	136,640 Mbits	6,832 Mbits	129,808 Mbits

I've allowed for a 5% reserve on the disc for a number of reasons. First, you will need the extra room to accommodate information that takes up disc space in the muxing process (.ifo control data files and .bup backup files). Second, even though they are small files, static menus and pictures do require space. Finally, the outside rim of the actual disc media is prone to problems and errors, so not packing the disc is in your best interest. (Note: Discs are written from the center out.)

Using common sense, with only 104 minutes of video footage, the feature and all the extras should logically be able to fit comfortably on a DVD-5. This is a sound rationalization and you could probably continue on without any more calculations, except for the fact that we still don't know the average bit rate to use to encode the video. We could certainly guesstimate but if you guess too high, there might not be enough space, and if you guess too low, you may sacrifice quality for no good reason.

The calculation is quite simple: It is the sum of the Total Bit Capacity of the DVD media minus the audio divided by the length of the combined video footage in seconds.

$$\frac{\text{Total Bit Capacity - Total Audio}}{\text{Total Video}} = \text{Average Bit Rate (Mbps)}$$

Let's apply this equation to the *Stranded* DVD.

DVD-5 = 35,720 Mbits
Total Audio = 3,807 Mbits
Total Video = 6,240 seconds

$$\frac{35,720 \text{ Mbits - } 3,807 \text{ Mbits}}{6,240 \text{ sec.}} = 5.11 \text{ Mbps}$$

Jot down that number (5.11 Mbps) and we'll put it to practical use in our next step.

▸ STEP 4: PREPARATION OF VIDEO

In order to use video in a DVD project it needs to be prepared. The first thing that needs to happen is to get it onto your computer. I don't care whether you shot it on 35mm, 16mm, 24p HD, PAL, DV, VHS, or even Super 8, if it's going to be part of your DVD, it needs to be converted into some kind of usable computer file.

Fortunately technology has gotten to the point where most of these formats are easily transferable. Provided you have the software, 24p HD, Digi-Beta, DV, and mini-DV cameras and decks can be plugged directly into the computer and captured. And with the use of an analog to digital converter, VHS can be transferred just as simply.

As far as film goes, unless you have your own personal film lab that you're keeping secret from the rest of the world, you'll probably need to take it to a professional service bureau to have it transferred. The telecine process converts the film into video and changes the frame rate from 24 fps (frames per second) to 29.97 fps, the standard for digital video.

Having limited funds, I decided to shoot *Stranded* on mini-DV at full frame and edit it on Final Cut Pro. My final result is a single uncompressed QuickTime (.mov) file.

This book assumes that you are familiar with the capturing and editing process. Even if you are not, understand that we are assuming that you already have your movie in an edited form on your computer, typically as an uncompressed QuickTime (.mov) file or AVID (.AVI) file. This is not to say that you can't output your movie to another format but that would suggest that you are having an outside lab do your encoding. In this book, we want to teach you to do it all yourself.

Before we continue, it's worth discussing two very important aspects of capturing that will impact the authoring of the DVD. They are *aspect ratio* and *video standard*.

ASPECT RATIO

This term refers to the length of the image versus its height. The standard television aspect ratios are 4:3 or 1.33:1 (also referred to as "full screen") and 16:9 or 1.78:1 (also referred to as "widescreen"). These are not to be confused with film aspect ratios which are 1:33:1 (Academy Aperture), 1.66:1 (European Widescreen), 1.85:1 (United States Widescreen), and 2.35:1 (Anamorphic Widescreen).

Many cameras offer both TV formats or offer lenses to achieve both. When you get to the authoring phase, you will need to decide whether the DVD will be one or the other, or both. Why this is so important is because a full frame picture will appear stretched on a widescreen TV and conversely a 16:9 image will need to be shrunk down and letterboxed (black bars on the top and bottom) in order to fit on a 4:3 screen.

VIDEO STANDARD

There are two major video standards in the world: NTSC (National Television Standards Committee) and PAL (Phase Alternating Line). They are both interlaced video formats but NTSC has a screen resolution of 720 x 480 pixels and a frame rate of 29.97 fps while PAL has a screen resolution of 720 x 576 pixels and a frame rate of 25 fps.

NTSC is the standard for North America as well as Japan, Central America, and most of South America and the Caribbean. PAL is used in Europe, Australia, New Zealand, Africa, the Middle East, and most of Asia.

DVD Studio Pro supports both standards, but for the purposes of our DVD project we will be dealing with NTSC. It's worth mentioning, though, that PAL has its advantages. Because of the extra bandwidth, Pal has a greater resolution and is closer to the look of film. It's also easier to transfer to film because of its frame rate of 25 fps versus the 24 fps of film.

Timecodes — There are two types of timecodes associated with NTSC video: Drop Frame and Non-Drop Frame. Timecodes are broken up into Hours:Minutes:Seconds:Frames and normal NTSC timecode is 30 fps while the actual NTSC video frame rate is 29.97 fps. In order to compensate, two frame numbers are dropped every minute except for the tenth minute. Thus Non-Drop Frame is 30 fps and Drop Frame is 29.97 fps. Unless you are using an older source material you will stick with Drop Frame Timecode.

VIDEO ENCODING

The next step requires us to transfer the video file into a useable DVD-compliant elementary stream. The preferred video language of DVD is the MPEG because it provides broadcast quality video at a data rate that is compliant with most industry standards. There are a few things you need to know about MPEG.

MPEG stands for "Moving Picture Experts Group," the company that developed this compression format.

Elementary vs. Multiplexed — The two most common types of MPEG streams are Elementary and Multiplexed. The Elementary contain only one stream (video or audio), while the Multiplexed combines both files into a single stream. DVD Studio Pro will only recognize the Elementary streams.

First, there are two types of MPEGs: MPEG-1 and MPEG-2.

The MPEG-1 video format is a lesser quality (352 x 240 compared to 720 x 480) and uses much lower data rates (maximum of 1.8 mbps) resulting in an inferior picture quality. The only plus about it is that you can fit more material on a DVD. Use this only if you aren't concerned with the appearance of the image. Otherwise, you should primarily be using the MPEG-2, which is the industry standard.

If your final movie was output to film then the best way to preserve the quality of the image is to skip the capturing altogether and encode straight from the film directly to the MPEG-2 format. This can be pricey though, and it must be encoded as an Elementary stream or it will not be useable in DVD Studio Pro.

Just as important as choosing the MPEG-2 is how the file will be encoded.

CBR VS. VBR ENCODING

There are two types of MPEG-2 encoding: CBR (Constant-Bit-Rate) and VBR (Variable-Bit-Rate). Although the names are more or less self-explanatory, I'll get a little more specific.

CONSTANT BIT RATE (CBR) ENCODING

With this type of encoding, you manually choose a Bit Rate that becomes the overall rate for the entire video file. Let's say that you choose a bit rate of 6.5 Mbps. This will mean that every second of the video file will have this bit rate, whether it needs it or not. The obvious drawback is that there will be frames that could have used a smaller rate while others may need more to display a clean image. Though this method generally takes less time, you wind up wasting valuable space on your DVD in the process.

Given that most encoders on the market now give you the option of using a variable bit rate, the CBR method of encoding is best used for talking heads, vintage footage, when you have a lot of extra disc space, or if you're just in a hurry.

VARIABLE BIT RATE (VBR) ENCODING

VBR encoding is a more intuitive method of encoding your footage and is crucial for footage with a lot of motion. By setting high and low rate limits, you allow a range of bit rates that is determined on a frame-by-frame basis. If a scene needs a low bit rate, it gets it and if needs a high one, well folks, it gets that too.

The greatest advantage to this process is that you are maximizing your DVD space by using the exact bit rate necessary to get the best look possible. The file size is the truest for your particular file. This is most helpful when you are trying to determine exactly how much of your material will ultimately fit on the DVD.

Now before you get all gung-ho about VBR, there's a little more to discuss. There are two types: One-Pass VBR and Two-Pass VBR

One-Pass VBR is just as it sounds, it compresses as it goes. The advantage is that it's certainly a step up from CBR encoding and, depending on the speed of your system, it's not extremely time-consuming. The drawback is that the ultimate file size may be larger than you might have anticipated.

Two-Pass VBR is much more accurate. The first pass determines the uniqueness of your particular video file and gives it an idea of where the highs and lows are. The second pass actually encodes the file based on this information. The advantage is obvious. Of course, this can take almost twice as long. So my advice, if you choose to do this, is to make sure that all your ducks are in a row before you click "begin encoding" and make damn well sure that you'll only have to encode it once.

To make matters even more complex, there are two types of encoders: hardware-based and software-based. The hardware-based type (like the Sonic encoder) requires an additional card in your computer, while the software-based (like the QuickTime MPEG Encoder or Media Cleaner) is just a program that can accomplish the encoding. The difference in quality is substantial, but so is the price difference. Most people will not be able to afford a hardware-based encoder and opt to take their footage to an outside lab with that capability. This makes sense if you shot your movie on film and want the best transfer possible, but if you shot it on video, these software-based encoders are more than adequate.

This is a lot of information to absorb, but it's vital to know. It actually breaks down into some very practical and easy decisions once you've sorted it all out.

Let's recap the choices:

>Full Screen (4:3) vs. Widescreen (16:9)
>NTSC (720 x 480) vs. PAL (720 x 576)
>MPEG-1 vs. MPEG-2
>CBR vs. VBR

Looking at it this way, it shouldn't seem so intimidating.

Full Screen (4:3) vs. Widescreen (16:9)

This simply depends on how you shot the movie.

NTSC (720 x 480) vs. PAL (720 x 576)

Simply ask yourself "Is my intended audience in North America or in Europe?"

MPEG-1 vs. MPEG-2

This is a gimme... You're crazy not to use MPEG-2.

CBR vs. VBR

It's a question of space and time (and we're not talking quantum physics). If you have the space, use CBR at a high bit rate. If you don't, but have the time, then use a two-pass VBR.

Now let's apply this to the *Stranded* DVD. As I mentioned, I shot the movie on mini-DV and edited it on Final Cut Pro. My final version was a single uncompressed QuickTime movie called "STRANDED Feature.mov."

Because I shot it full frame I'm going to keep it that way. My plan is to distribute it around Hollywood so NTSC it is. I want the best quality possible, but I know I'm dealing with space issues so my MPEG-2 will be encoded using a two-pass VBR. I'd rather take the time to do it right than sacrifice quality.

For this demonstration we will use the software-based QuickTime MPEG Encoder that comes with DVD Studio Pro 3. When installed it allows you the option of exporting MPEG-2s from any software you have that supports it, such as QuickTime Player and Final Cut Pro.

The MPEG-2 (.m2v) option will export files with a closed GOP pattern and a fixed GOP size (15 frames for NTSC and 12 frames for PAL). Audio files can be exported at the same time as a PCM Audio (.aiff). (See Step 5: Preparation of Audio.).

ENCODING THE STRANDED FEATURE

I will be encoding out of Final Cut Pro 4. This is in no way an endorsement of the software. It just happens to be the one I like to use, as well as being an industry leader in non-linear editing.

1) Select the file you want to encode. Our file is called STRANDED Feature.mov.

2) From the File pull-down menu select *Export* and from the Export pull-down menu select QuickTime (File > Export > QuickTime).

3) The Save dialogue box will appear and you should navigate to the Folders we set up in Step 1: Determining Your Assets. Choose the Main Feature folder in the Tracks folder. (DVD Book > Tracks > Main Feature). Next press the "Options" Button.

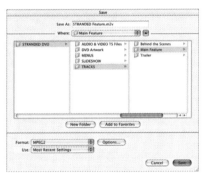

4.) The QuickTime MPEG-2 Exporter dialogue box will appear with the *Video* Tab displayed. Here we can choose the options that we decided on.

    Video Standard:

    Choose either NTSC or PAL. We want NTSC.

    Drop Frame: Because ours is 29.97 then we should select Drop Frame.

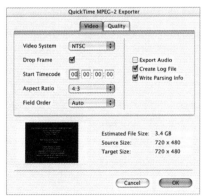

Start Timecode: We will start at 00:00:00:00 to match our video.

Aspect Ratio: Choose either 4:3 or 16:9. We want 4:3.

Field Order: Choose Auto to let the encoder make the appropriate choice.

Export Audio: Choose if you want to export the audio as an .aiff File.

Create Log File: Choose to create a text log with encoding and marker information.

Write Parsing Info: Choose to create the necessary parsing information that is utilized by DVD Studio Pro when importing files.

For our purposes, I have chosen to leave the Export Audio box unchecked. We will discuss audio further in Step 5: Preparation of Audio. Otherwise, feel free to check it on your projects.

5) Next select the *Quality* tab at the top of the dialogue box to display the Quality options. This dialogue box lets us set our bit rate and encoding type.

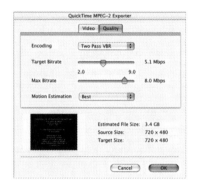

Encoding: Choose either One Pass, One Pass VBR or Two Pass VBR. Two Pass VBR.

Target Bit Rate: Using the slide, choose the bit rate we calculated (5.1 Mbps)

Max Bit Rate: I suggest a bit rate of 8 Mbps. Anything higher would be risky.

Motion Estimation: Choose either Good, Better or Best. I suggest Best. Even though it is slower, it will give you the highest quality possible with this encoder and reduce the amount of *artifacting*.

Artifacting — This term describes the imperfections you may see from time to time in your final image when it's viewed on a TV or computer monitor. It is particularly noticeable in the blacks. Unfortunately this is the nature of the beast. Anytime you transcode from one format to another, you will get artifacts. The only way to minimize their presence is to encode your video using the highest quality hardware and software you can get your hands on.

As you can see, the estimated file size is 3.4 GB. Not bad. That's still plenty of space to fit our other extras.

6) Press "OK" which will bring us back to the Save Dialogue box and then click the "Save" button. The encoding will immediately begin.

A new dialogue box will appear allowing you to track the progress of you MPEG-2 Export. As you can see, the encoder is estimating about nine hours to encode the roughly hour and a half of footage. This should

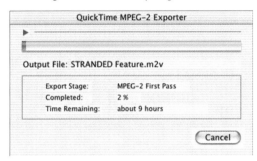

make it abundantly clear why you should do a bit budget. Finding out that this file doesn't fit when you are in the final stages of authoring would not only be annoying, it would also slow you down considerably, having to stop and re-encode the file at a lower bit rate.

If you click the triangle above the progress line, a preview window of the encoding will appear. This allows you to see what frame is being encoded at any particular time during the process. However, this will slow down the overall encoding process by about 20%. Meaning, in this case, it could take up to an additional two hours to finish.

Now that you are done with the Stranded Main Feature, you need to repeat the process for the other video assets: the Trailer and the Behind-the-Scenes Featurette. You will eventually have to do it for the Main Menu (motion menu); that will be discussed in Step 6: Preparation of Menus.

▸ STEP 5: PREPARATION OF AUDIO

Let's talk audio… I said LET'S TALK AUDIO! Sorry, I didn't know if you could hear me or not. Anyway, like video, audio encoding has its set of rules as well. The audio must be one of these types:

AUDIO FORMATS

> PCM Format
> AC-3 Dolby Digital
> MPEG-1, layer 2

PCM FORMAT

Pulse Code Modulation or linear PCM Format is an uncompressed format that is the basis for all digital audio. In order for the computer to use a recorded sound, it must make the transition from analog to digital. DVD specifications allow for mono or stereo PCM files with a 16-bit or 24-bit resolution and a sampling rate of either 48 kHz or 96 kHz. This format gives you the highest quality possible for your sound, but it also saddles you with a large file size with high bit rates that can compromise the bit rate of the accompanying video file. For example: A 16-bit, stereo PCM audio file at 48 khz has a bit rate of 1536 kbps and a 24-bit, stereo PCM audio file at 96 khz has a bit rate of 4608 kbps.

The typical kinds of uncompressed PCM files are:

AIFF (Audio Interchange File Format): Developed by Apple as a standard for their Macintosh computers. Recognized by its ".aif" extension.

WAV (Windows Application Format): Developed by IBM and Microsoft as a standard for PC audio. Recognized by its ".wav" extension.

SDII (Sound Designer II Format): Developed by Digidesign for its Sound Design editing software. Recognized by its ".sd2" extension.

AC-3 DOLBY DIGITAL

Developed by Dolby Laboratories, AC-3 is an attempt to bring movie theater-quality sound into the home theater arena. This format creates a close approximation of the original digital audio file by using a masking technique that throws away parts that can't be heard. The encoder analyzes the PCM signal and is able to determine which sounds are inaudible. By creating this hierarchy, it is able to discard extra sound data deemed unnecessary, thus being able to compress the file to a significantly smaller size (up to 12:1) than its original PCM format.

AC-3 has a considerably lower bit rate as well. A mono file has a bit rate between 64–128 kbps, stereo between 192–224 kbps, and 5.1 surround between 224–448 kpbs.

Once a perk, AC-3 decoders are now included on all DVD players, thus making the format the standard for audio sound. AC-3 also allows for up to six channels, making it possible to have true 5.1 sound — something PCM is entirely incapable of.

5.1 SURROUND SOUND

5.1 sound is an audio format that uses six discrete channels that pump the sound into five speakers (two front stereo speakers, one center speaker for dialogue, and two rear speakers for sound effects and music), plus a low-frequency subwoofer that literally creates a field that surrounds the viewer in sound.

MPEG AUDIO

The MPEG-1, layer 2 audio format is compatible with DVD specifications, but it is primarily used with PAL format DVD. Using it for NTSC projects can lead to incompatibility issues with certain DVD players. It surpasses AC-3 in the sense that it allows more audio channels (MPEG-1, layer 2 is capable of eight channels of audio) and it has a maximum bit rate of 912 kpbs compared to AC-3's 448 kbps. But even with these advantages, it is a rarely used format and therefore not recommended.

There are two additional audio formats worth mentioning:

DTS — Like AC-3, the Digital Theater System, or DTS audio format, was developed for movie theaters. It made its first appearance with Universal's Jurassic Park in 1993. The main difference between DTS and AC-3 is the compression method. AC-3 uses a compression ratio between 10:1 and 12:1 while DTS uses about 4:1, making it less compressed and supposedly giving clearer, crisper sound.

There is a debate over which format is better and it would seem that, based solely on technical specs, the DTS sound is better. The trade-off however is not in DTS's favor. The quality difference is so negligible that you would need to have top-of-the-line equipment to notice it, plus the size of DTS files are much bigger than those of AC-3. Most people would rather sacrifice the negligible difference in sound quality in order to save on disc space.

Another factor is that not all DVD players carry DTS decoders and you have to have a DTS player, a DTS receiver, and DTS-encoded DVD for it to all work. Also, the DTS software is expensive and not widely available at this time, making it even less attractive for low-budget production.

SDDS — Also developed for movie theaters, Sony Dynamic Digital Sound or SDDS uses ATRAC (Adaptive Transform Acoustic Coding) data reduction to produce a high-quality sound at one-fifth the file size of an uncompressed PCM file and is capable of 5.1 and 7.1 channels of surround sound. It has a sample frequency of 48 kHz and a max bit rate of 1280 kbps. Unfortunately it needs special equipment and eight speakers to reach its full effect. Also, it is not readily available for home use DVD at this point.

AUDIO ENCODING

Like video, in order to use audio in your DVD project it must be captured to your computer as well as synched up to your image before it can be encoded. It should be transferred uncompressed at 48 kHz (kilohertz) with 16-bit stereo. A 96 kHz sample rate can be used as well with 24-bit stereo, but for our purposes we'll stick with 48 kHz.

A common rookie mistake is to transfer at 44.1 kHz which is typically used for audio CDs. Make sure your settings are accurate because you'll just wind up wasting time later when you have to re-transfer all your audio.

Sound can be captured like video, it can be imported from CDs, or it can even be created on the computer itself. Whether you use one or all of these methods, the sound ultimately needs to be mixed and synched up to the video and in a useable format.

Once again, here are the bit rates for the most common audio formats used:

AUDIO FORMAT	BIT RATE
AC-3 2.0 Stereo	.192 Mbps
AC-3 5.1 Surround	.448 Mbps
16-Bit Stereo PCM (48kHz)	1.536 Mbps
24-Bit Stereo PCM (96kHz)	4.608 Mbps

This book presupposes that you are familiar with the techniques involved with capturing and mixing audio. Even if you are not, understand that we are assuming that you already have your mixed audio files as either AIFF, SoundDesigner II, QuickTime or WAVE files and are ready to proceed to the encoding process.

So let's pick up where we left off with the *Stranded* DVD.

Here are the audio files that make up the project:

Main Feature
Director's Commentary
Trailer
Behind-the-Scenes Featurette
Main Menu

As of now, all the files are saved as uncompressed PCM files in the AIFF format (16-bit/24 kHz). I have decided that I want to have the Main Feature Audio in 5.1 Dolby Digital Surround (AC-3) with all the other tracks in 2.0 Dolby Digital Surround. As an example, I've decided to leave the Main Menu as 16-bit, 48 kHz PCM stereo. (To be honest, in real life I would convert it to AC-3.)

The audio encoder we will be using is called A.Pack. Fortunately it is packaged with DVD Studio Pro and is quite simple to utilize.

Our files saved in the Tracks Folder should be as follows:

Main Feature Folder
> STRANDED-Feature.L.aiff
> STRANDED-Feature.R.aiff
> STRANDED-Feature.C.aiff
> STRANDED-Feature.Ls.aiff
> STRANDED-Feature.Rs.aiff
> STRANDED-Feature.SUB.aiff
> STRANDED-Comm.aiff

Behind the Scenes Folder
> STRANDED-Behind the Scenes.aiff

Trailer Folder
> STRANDED-Trailer.aiff

And in the Menus Folder:

Main Menu Folder
> MAIN MENU.aiff

Because I wanted the Main Feature to be in 5.1 surround sound, I was required to mix it in an outside sound editing program like Pro Tools, Logic, or Deck. The AC-3 encoder is not a sound mixing or editing program. It is just a compression tool that allows you to save space by altering the bit rate and file size. In order to achieve true surround sound you must divide the sound into the six separate channels. Otherwise you are just plugging in the same stereo tracks into the six channels and creating a simulated surround.

What follows is a step-by-step walkthrough of how to encode the "STRANDED-Comm.aiff" track into a 2.0 Stereo Dolby Digital (AC-3) file.

First thing to do is launch A.Pack.

1) The Instant Encoder dialogue box will appear. The left side of the box displays a graphical representation of the Audio Coding Mode. By default, it will be set for a 5.1 Coding Mode (3/2 (L, C, R, Ls, Rs) with the Enable Low Frequency Effects box checked). Each silver box represents a channel and, ultimately, a speaker. On the right side, the Audio tab is displayed. Before we continue, let's review some of the tab options:

AUDIO TAB

Target System: You are ultimately encoding the Audio for a DVD so leave this at the default.

Audio Coding Mode: Here is where you can choose different types of surround options ranging from 1/0 (C) which is mono

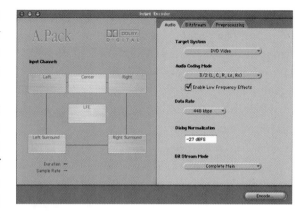

to 3/2 (L, C, R, Ls, Rs) which is 5.1 Surround. For the *Stranded* Commentary track we will choose 2/0 (L, R), which is stereo. The Enable Low Frequency Effects box is for a subwoofer and is unavailable for mono and stereo.

Data Rate: You can choose a data rate between 56 kbps and 448 kbps. For stereo, 192 kbps is quite sufficient while at 5.1, a rate of 448 kbps is suggested. Remember, the higher the rate, the better the quality.

Dialog Normalization: This number refers to the average volume of the dialogue within your sound file. The default is -27 dBFS. But I suggest setting it to -31 dBFS so your sound levels will not be altered during encoding.

Bit Stream Mode: Leave at the default of Complete Main. The other options are specific modes that are readable by some audio decoders.

BITSTREAM TAB

Center Downmix / Surround Downmix: These are only necessary if your encoded audio has these but your player does not. Leave at default settings.

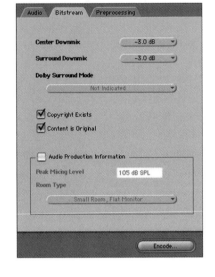

Dolby Surround Mode: In 2/0 mode you can specify Pro Logic. Leave at Not Indicated.

Copyright Exists: Check box if the audio is protected by copyright.

Content is Original: Check box unless the file is a copy.

Audio Production Information: With this section you can specify how the audio was mixed by entering the Peak Mixing Level and the Room Type. Unless you really know your stuff, leave this section alone.

PREPROCESSING TAB

Compression Preset: In almost all cases choose None. The default Film Standard Compression is only for a theatrical presentation.

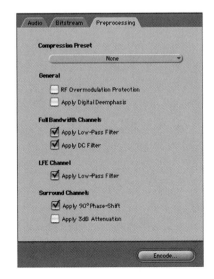

General: These should be left at their unchecked defaults.

Full Bandwidth Channels: These should be left at their checked defaults.

LFE Channel: Leave this checked unless the signal to the LFE's input is under 120 Hz.

Surround Channels: These should be left at their defaults; Apply 90° Phase-Shift should be checked, Apply 3dB Attenuation should be unchecked.

2) Using the Audio Coding Mode pull-down menu, select 2/0 (L, R). You will notice that the Enable Low Frequency Effects box will dim and become unavailable to select. Also the graphical display to the left will automatically change to represent the available channels. In this case we have only two channels available representing the left and right front stereo speakers of the television or surround system.

Using the Data Rate pull-down menu, select 192 kbps (the recommended rate for stereo). Finally, change the Dialog Normalization from -27 dBFS to -31 dBFS.

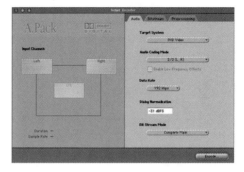

3) The next step requires you to select the files that are going to fill each channel. You might be wondering where the two channels come from, considering that we only have one file called "STRANDED-Comm.aiff." Because the Commentary was exported as a stereo PCM file, it already contains both the left and right channels.

There are two ways of importing the file. You can either select the left channel and a dialogue box will open allowing you to locate the file, or you can simply drag and drop the file onto the silver box.

4) A dialogue box will immediately appear, prompting you to choose which of the two file channels you want to utilize for this

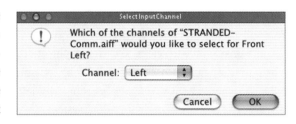

box. Fortunately, A.Pack assumes that for the left box you will want the left channel and it makes that the default option. This saves you the step of having to use the pull-down menu. This doesn't mean you *have* to select the left channel of the track, but I hope if you choose a different option that you have some compelling reason to do so. By doing this you are potentially altering the sound design of your movie, and sounds (based on the image) that should originate from the left would now appear to come from the right and could confuse the viewer or make the film just plain annoying to watch. Select OK and then repeat the process for the Right Box by selecting the right channel of the STRANDED-Comm.aiff file.

5.) You are now ready to encode. Click the Encode button located in the bottom right-hand side of the Instant Encoder dialogue box.

A new dialogue box will appear that prompts you for a destination for the encoded file (STRANDED-Comm. AC-3). I recommend saving it in the Main Feature Folder (Tracks > Main Feature).

Once you have selected the folder, click the Save button to begin the encoding.

6) The Progress dialogue box will appear with an estimated time for the encode.

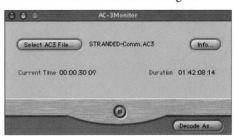

For this file, which is roughly 90 minutes long, the encoding will take just over 25 minutes. Unlike video encoding, audio encoding takes less time than the actual file length.

7) A.Pack has provided an AC-3 Monitor which allows you to test your AC-3 file. You can open the monitor by choosing it from the Windows pull-down menu (Windows > AC-3 Monitor).

The dialogue box will appear and prompt you to select a file to listen to. Click the button and navigate to and select our new file (STRANDED-Comm.AC-3). Press the play button and listen. An advantage to listening to the audio without the picture is that you are not distracted by the visuals, making it easier to focus on the nuances of the sound.

The AC-3 Monitor can also be used as a decoder, meaning you can choose an already existing AC-3 file and decode it back into a PCM file.

AUDIO CONCLUSION

Now that you've mastered the technique of encoding audio, you should repeat this process for the rest of your sound files.

The only major difference is when you encode the *Stranded* Main Feature audio. Because it is mixed in 5.1 you will have six channels to fill in the Instant Encoder. Be very careful when you are selecting each channel. It is very easy to get into a groove and not pay attention. If any one of those boxes has the wrong channel it will throw off your entire sound design and all that work will be for nothing.

I know I keep repeating myself, but it's worth saying more than once. Take the time to do it right the first time.

▸ STEP 6: PREPARATION OF MENUS

The menu, which is a screen with one or more buttons that allows the viewer to activate some function, is an essential component of a DVD. This graphic and text-based screen defines how you present your video information to the viewer.

The concept is very simple: Imagine going to a food establishment and having to guess at what they serve. Would you even stay for dinner?

Restaurant menus follow basic general principles, but each one is different. It's the same for DVDs. The menu will be based on the content and how you want to present it. If you want your DVD to have a classier feel, then having menus with clowns bouncing around and kazoo music chirping in the background may not be appropriate. The opposite is true as well: If your DVD is supposed to be loose and fun, a very stripped-down menu with a solid background color and white text may set an odd tone.

This is not to say you can't buck conventions, it just means that applying common sense to the menu design will certainly help rather than hinder. It all comes down to a very simple conceit: Good design is good *interface* design. Meaning, if it's obvious to the viewer how to navigate the menu, then you've done your job.

Navigation — A word that usually goes hand in hand with menu is "navigation," the act of steering or directing a course. When you "navigate" a DVD it means you are using the menus via the buttons to locate or "select" the content you are interested in viewing. Once an item is "selected" or "highlighted" it can then be "activated" with the press of a button.

In the past, our ability to navigate consisted of only a "Fast-Forward" and a "Rewind" Button. DVD allows for instant access and non-linearity, a concept that evolved from laserdisc technology and has been used for years in web-based design.

That said, you could very simply have only one menu with six buttons that allows you to access all of the content. There is nothing wrong with this scenario per se, but if you're trying to give your audience (i.e. the consumer) the biggest bang for their buck than you might want to put a little more effort into it. Which is the very essence of the concept of value-added content which we discussed earlier.

Believe it or not, many consumers feel cheated when they get only one menu, as if they didn't get their money's worth. On the other hand, don't go overboard. Some DVDs are absolutely labyrinthine in their navigation and it takes a degree in Advanced Cartography just to find the Play button. Once again defer to common sense in your navigation design. Remember that your Grandpa in the Midwest probably owns a DVD player by now and would appreciate not inducing an aneurism when trying to locate the Stills Gallery on the *Girls Gone Wild, Vol. 8* DVD.

There are two different types of DVD menus: Static Menus and Motion Menus. The Static Menu (or "Stills" Menu) has a picture or graphic for a background with either Layered Photoshop or Overlay Highlight buttons, while a Motion Menu has video and/or audio in the background and can only utilize the Overlay Highlight buttons.

Stills Menus with audio in the background are technically Motion Menus with a static background instead of a moving animation. This means that they are also subject to the same rules and limitations that apply to Motion Menus.

Our DVD project uses both Layered Photoshop Static Menus as well as a Motion Menu.

Here is a recap of the menus in the *Stranded* DVD:

STATIC MENUS

- ‣ Scene Selection Menu
- ‣ Special Features Menu
- ‣ Cast & Crew Bios Menu
- ‣ Director's Bio Menu
- ‣ Writer's Bio Menu
- ‣ Actor #1 Bio Menu
- ‣ Actor #2 Bio Menu

MOTION MENUS

Main Menu (with Audio)

Whether you are new to the world of DVD or are just brushing up on techniques, it's good to start with learning the basics of Static Menus first.

Static Menus

As mentioned before, there are two types of Static menus: Layered Photoshop menus or Overlay Highlight menus. Each has its advantages and disadvantages.

Layered Photoshop Menus

Layered Photoshop Menus allow for incredible flexibility with design and the use of high quality button graphics. The problem is that these types of menus take much longer to create and on the DVD itself, the buttons work much more slowly than Highlight Menus during selection and activation. Some designers (like myself) find this flaw to be an acceptable evil, feeling that the ability to push the boundaries graphically far outweighs the slower navigation.

Overlay Highlight Menus

Overlay Highlight Menus are much simpler to create and work like a breeze when you play the disc. The big disadvantage is that you are limited in your color palette and in your graphic capabilities. There is a reason, though, why this is the industry standard to designing menus. Many clever designers have found ways to circumvent the limitations and create menus on a graphical par with Layered Photoshop menus.

Before we jump into the creation of our menus, there is some important information you must know about how menus will appear in their final form on a television compared to how they look when you design them.

SQUARE PIXELS VS. NON-SQUARE PIXELS

Computers use square pixels (1:1 aspect ratio) while televisions use a non-square pixel (0.9:1 aspect ratio). When making your menus, you must compensate for the fact that computer screens represent images differently than TV monitors. If you don't, images created in Photoshop will appear slightly distorted when viewed on a television.

The solution is to create the menu at a larger resolution, then resize it before importing it into your authoring software.

NTSC MENUS

Aspect Ratio	Create	Resize
4:3 (Fullscreen)	720 x 534	720 x 480
16:9 (Widescreen)	854 x 480	720 x 480

PAL MENUS

Aspect Ratio	Create	Resize
4:3 (Fullscreen)	768 x 576	720 x 576
16:9 (Widescreen)	1,024 x 576	720 x 576

VIDEO SAFE & TITLE SAFE ZONES

Another important consideration is that your menus are subject to the same spatial limitations as video. And because every television is different, a button may appear to be right on the edge of the frame on some TVs, but be cut off (and not visible) on others.

The best advice is to keep the television's Video (or "Action") Safe and Title Safe Zones in mind and keep your graphics, text, and especially your buttons well within these areas.

VIDEO/ACTION SAFE ZONE

This is a rectangular area that is located 5% in from the edges. So for 4:3 NTSC it would be 36 pixels in on the left and right edges (5% of 720 pixels) and 24 pixels in from the top and bottom edges (5% of 480 pixels).

TITLE SAFE ZONE

This is a rectangular area that is located 10% in from the edges. So for 4:3 NTSC it would be 72 pixels in on the left and right edges and 48 pixels in from the top and bottom edges.

Remember when setting up your Title and Action Safe areas to compensate for the different resolution sizes for NTSC and PAL and for 4:3 and 16:9. Also remember to take into account the fact that you are creating the menus at a different resolution size and then resizing them.

As far as pixel density goes, you can create your menus at whatever resolution you desire, but the industry standard is 72 ppi (pixels per inch). While you can choose any resolution you want for menus, this doesn't apply to ".pict" files (the format used for DVD still images). They *must* be 72 ppi, so you might as well keep everything at this resolution.

MAKING A LAYERED PHOTOSHOP MENU

Now let's create a menu. For this demonstration we'll make the *Stranded* Scene Selection Menu. Before we even touch the computer we need to think about what this menu needs to accomplish. First let's list the buttons we will need:

SCENE SELECTION MENU BUTTONS

- ‣ Chapter 1: Vacation
- ‣ Chapter 2: Dumped
- ‣ Chapter 3: Hitchin'
- ‣ Chapter 4: Despair
- ‣ Chapter 5: Realization
- ‣ Chapter 6: Homecoming

There is one more button missing from this list: "Return to Main Menu" or just plain "Main Menu." Nine times out of ten you may forget to include this button when you are making your menus; even though it is obvious, it never seems to be the first thing on your mind. Remind yourself that for viewers to be able to navigate through your DVD, they need to be able to get back to the Main Menu or at least the sub-menu that got them there. Including this button, this gives us a total of seven buttons.

Now that we know what the menu needs to accomplish, we need to consider how we want to graphically display this. My advice is to think about the context of the movie.

A simple solution is to grab a frame from the movie, use that as the background, throw on some text and be done with it.

Frame Grab — Using Final Cut Pro, you have the ability to export a single frame from your project and use it as part of your menus or as the entire background. You simply locate the frame you want on the timeline and Choose Export as a QuickTime in the File pull-down menu (File > Export > QuickTime). In the Dialogue box choose Still Image in the Format pull-down menu (Format > Still Image). Select the Option Button to specify the file format and the frame rate of the movie file (in most cases 29.97 fps). Save it and you are ready to go.

There's nothing wrong with that. But for our purposes I'm going to propose something a little more abstract that I think you'll like and that might get the juices flowing when you consider the types of menus you'll design for your projects in the future.

Since *Stranded* is about a woman making a cross-country trek and the different chapters represent different points of her journey, why not use some kind of a map as a background for the Scene Selection Menu? The different chapters could be points along the map that either literally mark her progress or somehow suggest it. I can already see the possibilities and it gives my DVD a little more charm than the standard frame grab with text.

THE BACKGROUND

First, launch Adobe Photoshop. I suggest using the latest version of the program. This menu was created using Version 7.0.

From the File drop-down menu Select New (File > New). A dialogue box will appear. Click on the Preset Sizes drop-down menu and select 720 x 534 Std. NTSC DV/DVD.

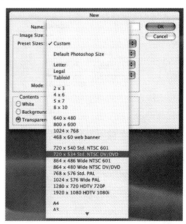

Next, type in a name in the Name Field. We chose to call it "Sc. Selection MENU." Make sure the Mode is set for RGB Color.

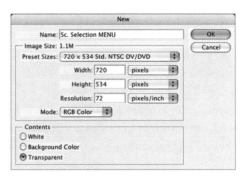

You will now have a blank canvas to work with. I suggest that you take this opportunity to set up your Action and Title Safe guides. The easiest way to do this is to open Photoshop Preferences and select Units & Rulers (Preferences > Units & Rulers). In the Units & Rules Dialogue box, use the Rulers pull-down menu in the Units section to change the meas-urements into percent. Make sure that the Rulers are visi-

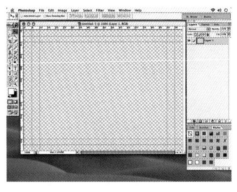

ble (View > Rulers) and, using the move tool, drag Guides (top, bottom, left and right) into the 5% areas for Action Safe and 10% areas for Title Safe.

A way to save time on future projects is to take this one step further. Using the Line Tool, draw two black (3 pixels wide) rectangles to represent each of the Safe Zones. Merge those layers separate from the background and name the Layer "Safe Guides." Save this document as a .psd file called "720 X 534 Guides.psd." Now anytime in the future you want to make a new menu you can import this layer and instantly have the guides at your disposal.

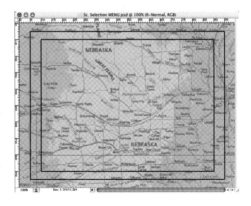

As mentioned above, I wanted to use some kind of map in the background. The simplest solution is to either buy one and scan in the picture or download one from the internet (if you choose either of these options, make sure that using the image does not infringe copyright). I found a map to use and brought it in as the background. Because it's such a busy graphic, I lowered its opacity to 90%. I've also left the guides as the topmost layer, leaving them visible so I don't forget. It's best to not turn them off until you are finished.

Next I want to add one more element to my background: some text that lets viewers know that they are on the right menu (i.e. Scene Selection).

As a rule of thumb with text you want to use a sans-serif font, 18 points or higher. Not only will this make the text easier to read, it will also reduce the "flicker" effect.

Flicker — This is a strobe-like quality which can make the text difficult to read as well as be hard on the viewer's eyes. Using sans-serif fonts as opposed to serif fonts can greatly reduce this problem. The flicker can also affect graphics as well. Thus it's not recommended to use horizontal lines that are 3 pixels or less in width.

I've decided to use 24-point Arial Bold in blue. Using the Layer Styles, I've also applied a 2-point black stroke and a drop shadow to separate it from the background and make it pop a little better.

To finish the background you should combine the map and text into one layer using the "Merge

Down" Function. To do this select the Text Layer in the Layers Palette and choose "Merge Down" from the Layers pull-down menu (Layers > Merge Down). Rename the new layer "Background." The Guides should still be a separate layer.

I highly recommend saving the unmerged document as a separate file using the "Save As" option in the File Pull-Down Menu (File > Save as). I can't tell you how many times I've wanted to go back to the original Layers to tweak them slightly, either for aesthetic reasons or because something was being cut off on the TV. It's better to be safe than sorry, sorry meaning having to start over from scratch.

THE BUTTONS

Every button should have three distinct layers or "States." They are Normal, Selected (or Highlighted), and Activated.

The Normal state is the default state. It is the button as it appears when it is neither selected nor activated by the viewer.

The Selected state is the appearance of the button when the viewer highlights the texts. This is to let the viewer know where they are as they scroll down the possible choices. This can consist of a simple change of text color or an underline, or it can be as elaborate as an overlayed picture or an extreme change in the text.

The third button layer is the Activated state. This layer is only seen for a split second when the viewer presses the enter button on the remote. This layer can be radically different from both previous layers or it can be as simple as going back to the original Normal state of the button.

The great thing about Photoshop is that you are limited only by your imagination. Feel free to think as far out of the box as you wish, keeping in mind that the menu is a navigational device (or table of contents) for the viewer. If you get out there too far it may lead to confusion. Believe it or not, keeping it too simple can lead to confusion as well.

Two-Button Confusion — If you have only two buttons, you have only two choices. So let's say that the two buttons are "Play Movie" and "Scene Selection" and the menu designer chose yellow text as the Normal layer, green text as the Selected layer, and blue text as the Activated layer. When you get to this Menu the word "Play Movie" will be green (because one button must be selected at all times) and the word "Scene Selection" will be yellow (its Normal State). If I press any navigation button on the DVD remote, the "Play Movie" button will turn yellow and the "Scene Selection" button will turn green. Follow me so far?

Here's the question: As the viewer, how do I know that Yellow = Normal and Green = Selected? The designer could just as easily have chosen Green = Normal and Yellow = Selected and, guess what, the menu would look exactly the same.

Toggling back and forth between the buttons will only get you even more confused. If you had a third button, you'd just use process of elimination, but with two, you don't have that option. The only recourse is to press the "Enter" button on the DVD remote and hope that you are actually selecting the button you want.

The solution to this is fairly easy. Make the button States obvious. If you have a two-button menu, then use a simple underline, box, or dot next to the button to denote its Selected layer. If you want to be fancy about it, have the text get larger or have a glow around the text when it's highlighted.

PHOTOSHOP EFFECTS LAYERS

With its Layer Styles options, Photoshop allows you to alter your text and graphics in many creative ways. These options can really up the visual quality of your DVD menus. It's perfectly acceptable to use these Photoshop Effects Layers provided that you flatten the individual layer before you import it into your authoring software. Unless you do, DVD Studio Pro will not recognize Effects Layers, Transfer Modes, and Layer Styles when they are imported.

For example: This "Play Movie" button has its three layers set up. I've decided that I want the Selected layer to have an Outer Glow and a Bevel and Emboss Effect. First, select the Layer in the  Layers Palette and choose "Blending Options" from the Layer Style pull-down menu in the Layers pull-down menu (Layers > Layer Styles > Blending Options).

The Layer Style dialogue box will appear. Choose "Outer Glow" and "Bevel and Emboss" from the list. Feel free to adjust these with the advanced controls as you see fit.

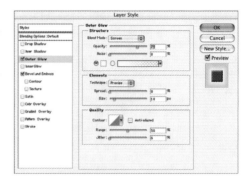

Press "OK" and you're ready to continue.

The Layers Palette should now reflect the Effect Layers you chose and your Selected Layer should look something like this.

As I mentioned before, the authoring software will not recognize these Effects Layers as they currently are. But if you flatten the individual layer it will.

This is not the same as Flattening the Image. If you chose this function ("Flatten Image"), it will combine all your Layers into one Layer and completely defeat the purpose.

The first thing you need to do is to add a new Layer in your Layer Palette (Layer > New > Layer) and position it directly below the "PLAY-Selected" Layer.

Next either choose "Merge Down" from the Layer Pull-Down Menu (Layer > Merge Down) or turn off all the other Layers in the Layers Palette (besides "PLAY-Selected and Layer 1). Select "PLAY-Selected" and choose "Merge Visible" from the Layer pull-down menu (Layer > Merge Visible). If you use "Merge Down" you'll need to rename the layer.

BUTTONS: NORMAL STATE

As said before, the "Normal" State represents the look of the button when it is in default mode. I've decided that it might be interesting to lay out my chapters as if they were points on this hypo-thetical map.

To accomplish this I cre-ated seven new layers of text. The font I chose was 18-point Arial Bold and the color white (except for the Main Menu text, where I used green to visually separate it from the other selections).

As you can see, I also added some Layer Styles to my text to make it stand out from the background a little better. I used a black 1-point stroke and a drop shadow, then I flattened each individual layer as discussed in the Photoshop Effects Layers section.

I suggest taking the time to rename the layers as you complete each step. We have seven buttons, which will require three layers each plus the background and guides. This is a total of 23 layers, which doesn't include the Divider Layers.

Divider Layers — DVD Studio Pro has a way to help you organize your Photoshop Layer menu buttons so that when you get into authoring it's a little easier on the eyes. If you create new layers that are labeled " - " (the minus sign) and use these lay-

ers to separate the sets of button layers (a set being Normal, Selected, and Activated Layers), the software will automatically divide the sets into sec-tions that are visually easier to deal with.

Name the Layers "1-Normal," "2-Normal," "3-Normal," "4-Normal," "5-Normal," "6-Normal," and "MAIN-Normal." When you are done your Layers Palette should look like this.

When creating buttons like these, it is wise to wait until all your layers are created before you start merging layers. This makes it easier to make changes to buttons. It can also speed up the process quite a bit because you have the ability to duplicate layers and make adjustments, instead of having to start from scratch every time you create a new layer.

Save the file and we are now ready to move onto the next step.

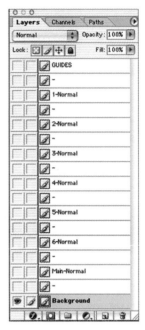

BUTTONS: SELECTED STATE

Now it's time to move onto the next set of layers, the Selected State. This layer must be different from the Normal state of the button or the viewer will have no idea that they have highlighted it. In web design, this is called the Roll-Over State.

We could simply have the text change color, but if we were doing that there would be no reason to do this as a Photoshop Layer menu. That kind of effect can be achieved much more easily using Overlay Highlight menus (see section on Overlay Highlight Menus).

For this design, I thought about icons that might be associated with maps. Something immediately popped into my head: push-pins. How many times have you seen these multicolored pins pressed into a map to mark locations? What better a way to show a selected layer than to put a pin through it.

The first step is to create the push-pin itself. I opened up a new Photoshop file the same size as the menu file (720 x 534) with a 72 ppi resolution and saved it as "Push-Pin.psd."

Using the pencil, I drew a simple push-pin shape. Then, utilizing the Layer Styles, I added some texture and a drop shadow. Next I made different colored variations to choose from.

Next, I created seven new layers by cutting and pasting the various colored push-pins into the Scene Selection menu.

Using the Scale and Rotate options in the Transform pull-down menu (Edit > Transform > Scale, Edit > Transform > Rotate) I was able to size and position the pins at various angles.

I then used the Move Tool to position them so that they would look like they were sticking into the different selections.

Now that they are all in position and I like the placement and the look, I need to name the Layers: "1-Selected," "2-Selected," "3-Selected," "4-Selected," "5-Selected," "6-Selected," "MAIN-Selected." At this point, your Layers Palette should look like this.

BUTTONS: ACTIVATED STATE

The Activated State is the final layer set. As mentioned before, this is the layer that is only seen when the viewer actually makes a selection. Depending on how fast the DVD player is, it may only be visible for a second or so.

For this layer set, I considered doing a stroke around the push-pin or a glow, but neither worked well. Because there are so many pin colors, finding the right stroke color was problematic and the glow didn't show up well with the light-colored map background. Besides, I wanted to be a little more clever than that.

Another common image associated with maps is "X marks the spot." So it occurred to me to have a giant "X" appear right in the center of where the push-pin was.

Because I wanted the push-pin graphic to still be part of the layer, I needed to duplicate the graphic first. This gets us to an important issue about Photoshop Layered Menus. You must understand how DVD Studio Pro treats these layers. They are all separate from each other and are swapped out. In other words, when the Normal Layer is displayed, the Selected and Activated are hidden. When the Selected Layer is displayed, the Normal and Activated are hidden, and when the Activated Layer is displayed, the Normal and Selected Layers are hidden.

This means that if you want the Normal layers to always be visible (as we do in this menu), they must either be *assigned* to every layer or they must be *incorporated* into each layer.

You have both options when you get to the authoring stage, but I find it is easier and more effective to adjust the layers in Photoshop than having to remember to check multiple items per each layer. (More on that in Section IV: Authoring the DVD.)

To create the Activated Layers, as mentioned before, I first duplicated each push-pin. This is done by selecting the layer and choosing Duplicate Layer from the Layer pull-down menu (Layer > Duplicate Layer).

Next I created a new layer and, using the Text Tool, wrote the letter "X" in red. I beefed up the letter and applied a stroke and a glow to give it a little kick to it. Once I was satisfied with the look of the "mark," I duplicated it six times and, using the Move Tool, positioned all of them in the center of each push-pin.

Because they are Effects Layers, I need to flatten them individually. Fortunately, I can kill two birds with one stone because they also need to be combined with the duplicated push-pin layers. Doing that will automatically rasterize the effect.

Once they are all merged, they should be renamed: "1-Activated," "2-Activated," "3-Activated," "4-Activated," "5-Activated," "6-Activated," "MAIN-Activated." When you are done, your Layers Palette should look like this.

There is still the problem of the Normal layer of the text. As mentioned before, we can assign these layers in DVD Studio Pro to always be visible or I can simply merge them onto the background and save myself all that work later.

I once did a DVD with fourteen menus. Each menu had an average of seven buttons. Do the math. That's 7 buttons x 3 layers x 14 menus = 294 boxes I had to check. And that's being conservative with the numbers. You always want to make it easier on yourself when you get to the authoring stage. There are so many things to keep track of. Any chance to minimalize the work is in your best interest.

To do this, turn off all the layers except the Normal layers and the background. Select the background layer and choose Merge Visibles from the Layers pull-down menu.

At this point you are almost done with the menu. There are just a few finishing touches that you need to do before you can move on to your other work.

FINALIZE THE MENU

It's crucial at this point to make sure you are happy with your menu. Is the background too overwhelming, thus obscuring the buttons? Do you like the different button states? Is the navigation clear? Is everything in the Title Safe area?

Once you have given the menu the once-over, I suggest saving it as the raw menu. (i.e. Sc. Selection Menu(Raw).psd). This way if you have unforeseen changes down the road, you can at least start with this menu as opposed to having to start from scratch. It has been my experience that I've needed this version of the menu for almost every project I've done.

NTSC FILTER

When working with menus that have frame grabs, it's wise to apply an NTSC Filter to the finished menu. This will greatly help to compensate for the interlace flicker that you can get with these images in particular. Simply choose NTSC from the Filter pull-down menu (Filter > Video > NTSC).

GAUSSIAN BLUR

The best way to compensate for interlace flicker on menus with heavy text is to apply a 1% Gaussian Blur to your finished menu. It is located in the Blur pull-down menu in the Filter pull-down menu (Filter > Blur > Gaussian Blur).

A dialogue box will prompt you to choose a pixel radius. Select "1.0" on the slide bar and then click OK to complete.

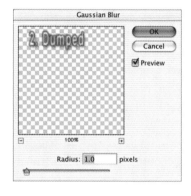

Repeat this for all your text layers.

RESIZE AND SAVE: THE FINAL STEP

Now before you start patting yourself on the back, don't forget the most important step of all. Drumroll please…

Resizing the menu.

Remember way back when I mentioned square pixels and non-square pixels? Sound vaguely familiar? Well, this is where that comes into play.

Fortunately, this couldn't be any easier. All you need to do is choose Image Size from the Image pull-down menu (Image > Image Size).

The dialogue box will appear. Uncheck the Constrain Properties box (if it's checked) and then type in 480 where it says 534. Click "OK" and watch the magic happen.

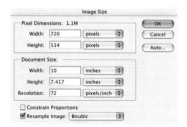

When you're done it will now look like this. Save this file as Sc. Selection MENU.psd.

Under no circumstances should you Flatten the entire image or save it as anything but a .psd file.

MAKING A STATIC OVERLAY MENU

As mentioned before, there is another method of creating button layers, using an Overlay Highlight Menu. These typically take less time to create and author, but once again they have their limitations. That's not to say that you are whimping out by doing it this way because most DVDs on the market utilize this type of menu. So if it's good enough for the big kids...

There are two different kinds of overlays: Simple and Advanced. Simple overlays only utilize one color while Advanced overlays may use up to four colors, which allows for a little more control over the look of your button highlights.

For the purpose of demonstrating a Static Overlay Highlight menu, I'm going to use a Simple overlay. We will discuss Advanced overlays in the next section which is dedicated to the creation of a Motion Menu.

This by no means suggests that you can't use an Advanced overlay on a Static Menu or Simple overlays on a Motion Menu.

Getting back to the *Stranded* DVD, I've decided that we will use one of the Cast & Crew Bio pages as a good way to teach this method. I've chosen to create the Director's Bio menu.

CREATING A STATIC SIMPLE OVERLAY MENU

Begin as before by launching Adobe Photoshop and opening up a new document.

From the File drop-down menu select New. A dialogue box will appear.

Click on the Preset Sizes drop-down menu and select 720 x 534 Std. NTSC DV/DVD.

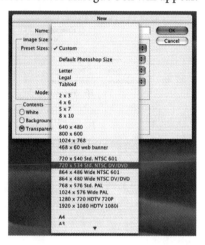

A dialogue box will appear. Type in a name in the Name Field. We will call it "C&C MENU-Sebastian S." Finally, make sure the Mode is set for RGB Color.

Click OK to continue.

You will now have a blank canvas to work with.

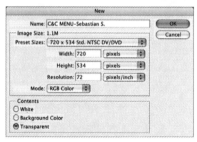

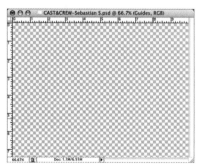

Continuing with our "map" theme, I decided to use a different type of map as the background for our Cast & Crew Bios menus. I also dropped the opacity down to 30% to reduce boldness.

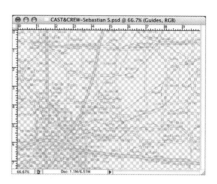

As before, make sure that everything is in the TV Title Safe area. Remember when I had you save the guides earlier? This is how that can come in handy. Just find that file and cut and paste that layer into this new document.

If you didn't, however, now you will need to recreate them. Once again, make sure that the measurements are set to percent by selecting Units & Rulers (Preferences > Units & Rulers). In

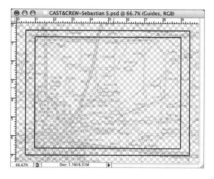

the Units & Rulers Dialogue box, use the Rulers pull-down menu in the Units section to change the measurements into percent. Make sure that the Rulers are visible (View > Rulers). Using the move tool, drag Guides (top, bottom, left, and right) into the 5% areas for Action Safe and 10% areas for Title Safe. Creating a menu 720 x 534, the NTSC Title Safe areas are 72 pixels in on the left and right sides and 54 pixels in on the top and bottom. Use Ruler Guides to set these parameters.

Next, I create new layers and add text and a picture. Because this is a biography of the director I thought it might be a nice touch to include his credits. To make the body of the text really stand out from the background, I used black text with a yellow Outer Glow and a Drop Shadow. I also added a 2-point black stroke around the picture with a Drop Shadow as well.

Because this is a menu, we need to have buttons. For this menu I will need two buttons: a "Back" button to go to the previous menu (in this case the Cast & Crew Bios menu) and a "Next" Button. This is used to continue to the next Bio menu (Producer's Bio) instead of having to go back to the Bios menu and select it from there. In essence, I'm saving the viewer a step, but still giving options.

BUTTON HIGHLIGHTS

We now need to create the Overlay that can be authored to display the Selected and Activated states of the buttons. The easiest way to show that an option is selected is by having an underline appear below the text. Given the fact that we have only two buttons, I'm going to recommend this method.

Start by creating a new Layer (Layer > New > Layer) and making sure it's positioned at the top of the Layers Palette. Using the Line Tool draw a 9-point black line directly underneath the word "Back" about the length of the word. Repeat this process under the word "Next".

Create another new Layer (Layer > New > Layer) and place it underneath the previous layer in the Layers Palette. Use the Fill Tool to fill that layer with white.

Because there are three other Bio menus to make, I highly recommend saving the unflattened document at this point as a separate .psd file using the Save As option in the

File pull-down menu (File > Save as). Call it BIO MENU-Template. This way you can create the rest of your Bio menus quite easily by swapping out the pictures and the text and saving them as their own files. This will save you an enormous amount of time because you won't have to start from scratch every time.

At this point you have seven layers representing your background (Title, Body Text, Filmography, Picture, Back Button, Next Button, and Background) and two layers representing your overlay (the Underlines and the white background).

Turn off the Overlay layers (and the Guides layer) and use the Merge Visible option (Layers > Merge Visible) to combine the layers. Rename this new layer "Background." Next turn off the new Background layer and merge

the two Overlay layers (Layers > Merge Visible). Rename the new layer "Overlay."

Delete the Guides layer and you are left with the two layers that you need in order to author your menu.

RESIZE THE IMAGE

The next step requires you to resize the menu to the correct proportions for the DVD. We began with the size 720 x 534 and we now want to resize it to 720 x 480. Do this by selecting Image Size from the Image pull-down menu (Image > Image Size).

A dialogue box will appear. Uncheck the Constrain Properties box (if it's checked) and then type in 480 in the Height Field where it currently says 534.

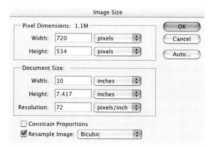

Click OK to continue and the document will be resized.

SAVE AS A PICT OR PHOTOSHOP FILE

The last step is to save your completed menu. You actually have a few options. You could leave it as a layered Photoshop document (.psd). The layers must be two separate flattened layers. You could also save it as two individual flattened Photoshop files. i.e. Bio-Sebastian S.(Background).psd and Bio-Sebastian S.(Overlay).psd.

The third option is to save it as two individual PICT Files (.pct). First separate the layers into two flattened Photoshop files: Bio-Sebastian S.(Background).psd and Bio-Sebastian S.(Overlay).psd.

Start with Bio-Sebastian S.(Background).psd. Choose Save As from the File pull-down menu (File > Save As). The Save As dialogue box will appear. Using the Format pull-down menu, choose "PICT File" (Format > PICT File).

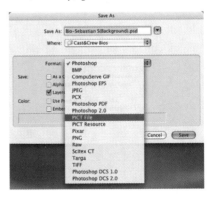

The PICT File Options dialogue box will appear. Under Resolution, select "32 bits/pixel" and in the Compression section select "None". Click OK to continue.

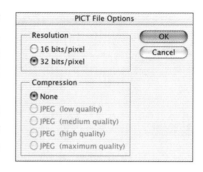

Save the PICT file: Bio-Sebastian S. (Background).pct in the Cast & Crew sub-folder we created in the MENUS folder.

Repeat this process for Bio-Sebastian S.(Overlay).psd.

MAKING A MOTION OVERLAY MENU

Making Motion menus is very similar to making the Static Overlay menus. The one big difference is that instead of using a still image as the background you are using a video file. Motion menus add a lot to your overall DVD project and can really enhance the experience for your viewer.

DVD designers spend many hours coming up with complex animations for use in menus and ultimately try to out-do big-name titles.

Now as attractive as it seems to jump into doing all motion menus, it is time-consuming and, most importantly, it takes up more space on your DVD that might take the place of honest-to-goodness content.

That said, I've decided to do my main menu for the *Stranded* DVD as a motion menu. It seems appropriate and I feel it gives my project a little more merit. Forgive my insecurities.

I also want to use advanced overlays for my button highlights.

The first thing we need to do is decide what the menu is going to be. So far we've been using maps to tie into the theme of our movie. For this menu I thought it would be interesting to show a lonely highway with maybe some passing cars. This suggests the journey, but also the main character's isolation.

At this point I have two options. I could search through the movie and see if I can use any scenes from the movie or find something outside the film that could work (once again keep in mind possible copyright infringements).

I found some footage from my movie of the main character walking down the middle of a road that lasts for about two minutes. Considering that a reasonable length for a motion menu (which before it loops is between 30 seconds to a minute long), it looks like I have the video footage I need.

ADDING THE BUTTONS

Like the Static Overlay menus, the Normal button states must be incorporated into the background, in this case the video. In other words you are going to need to composite text into the video footage. There are a number of programs that will allow you to do this, the most popular being Final Cut Pro and Adobe After Effects.

Whichever program you decide to choose, this book is going to assume that you understand compositing techniques. Remember that it is of outmost importance that any titles, logos, and especially button text remain within the Title Safe area of the image.

The *Stranded* DVD Main Menu consists of three options: Play Feature, Scene Selection, and Special Features. You will probably also want to incorporate the title of the movie as well.

Because I didn't want to have just plain text over the image, I decided to add some graphic quality to it as well. I also shifted the movie image so it is in the upper left hand part of the frame.

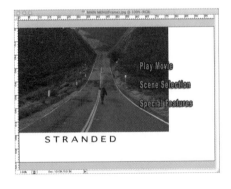

Once you have the text composited into the video footage and have added any music or sound that you may want, you need to do two things.

First, you will need to do a frame grab in order to have a guide to make your overlay. As we discussed earlier, locate a frame on the timeline and choose Export as a QuickTime in the File pull-down menu (File > Export > QuickTime). In the dialogue box choose Still Image in the Format pull-down menu (Format > Still Image). Select the Option button to specify the file format and the frame rate of the movie file (in most cases 29.97 fps). Save it and you're ready to go.

Once you have the Overlay reference frame, you can export the video footage as an MPEG-2 (see Step 4: Preparation of Video) and any audio as an AIFF file (see Step 5: Preparation of Audio).

PREPARING THE REFERENCE FRAME

Launch Photoshop and locate and open the Main Menu Overlay Reference Frame (File > Open). Because the frame is a video file it is already at the correct size (720 x 480). You will need to resize it to 720 x 534 in order to make the overlay. Otherwise they will not line up when they are authored in DVD Studio Pro.

Select Image Size from the Image pull-down menu (Image > Image Size).

A dialogue box will appear. Uncheck the Constrain Properties box (if it's checked) and then type in 534 in the Height Field where it currently says 480.

Click OK to continue and the document will be resized. Save this document as MAIN MENU Reference.psd in my Main Menu Folder (MENUS > Main Menu).

BUTTON HIGHLIGHTS

We now need to create the overlay that can be authored to display the Selected and Activated states of the buttons. In the previous menu we used Simple overlays to create lines underneath the text. For the Main Menu, I wanted to be a little more creative. I thought that using highway signs might be an interesting approach and I'm not going to limit myself to one sign either.

Here's what I decided:
- ▸ Play Movie — Speed Limit Sign
- ▸ Scene Selection — No U-turn Sign
- ▸ Special Features — Keep Right Sign

For these kind of button highlights I'm going to have to use Advanced Overlays.

ADVANCED OVERLAYS

As mentioned before, Advanced Overlays allow you to use up to four colors to represent the button highlight. There are also two methods to create them: Chroma and Grayscale. Chroma utilizes the colors white, red, blue, and black, while Grayscale uses black (0%), dark gray (33%), light gray (66%), and white (100%).

MAKING AN ADVANCED OVERLAY

The first thing we'll do is create the road signs. Open a new 720 x 534 document with an empty background in Photoshop. (Even though this is more space than you'll need, this will guarantee that the proportions stay consistent when you cut and paste them into the Frame Reference document.)

I've decided to make the road sign graphics using the chroma method (white, red, blue, black). To make it easier to create them, I've drawn them oversized but consistent in size to one another.

Fortunately, I chose graphics that utilize only three colors: white for the sign; black for the borders, graphics and text; and red on the No U-Turn sign. Because the color white will also be incorporated as the background color of the entire document and we need the background to be transparent, we need to use the fourth color (blue) to represent the white parts of the signs.

Remember, technically these are all placeholder colors. You choose the actual highlight colors in DVD Studio Pro. In other words, even though the sign color is now blue, when you author it you will instruct blue to represent white.

Using the fill tool, change the white to blue.

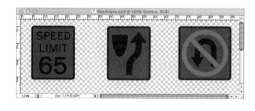

Save this document as Roadsigns.psd in the Main Menu Folder (MENUS > Main Menu).

Going back to our MAIN MENU Reference.psd document, cut and paste the road signs as three individual new layers. Using the Transform pull-down menu, select Scale and resize them to a more manageable size (Edit > Transform > Scale).

Using the Move tool, place them next to their respective text: Play Movie = Speed Limit Sign, Scene Selection = No U-Turn Sign, Special Features = Keep Right Sign.

I chose to place them to the left of the text so that there was no chance they would get cut off on the right side.

Save the document and rename it MAIN MENU (Overlay).psd (File > Save As).

At this point we don't need the background anymore. Feel free to either turn off the layer or delete it from the document altogether. Making sure that all three road sign layers are selected, merge the three layers into one (Layers > Merge Visible.

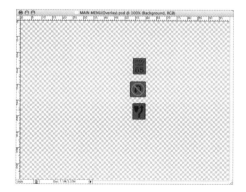

Now that you are finished with the overlay, you need to resize it to the original proportions of the video which is 720 x 480 (Image > Image Size).

Finally, save the document and it is ready for importing into the authoring software.

Using the Overlay and assigning Highlight Colors will be discussed in the next chapter.

ALTERNATE METHODS: ANTI-ALIASED TEXT AND GRAPHICS

There is another method of doing highlights that utilizes the Advanced Overlays to simulate soft edges on both text and graphics. This is a much more complex process and can lead to some funky results if not done properly. But, that said, it is also the industry standard for doing Advanced Highlight menus and is worth learning whether you choose to utilize it or not.

Let's go back in time and approach our Main Menu from a different angle. Instead of road signs, I've decided that I want Highlights directly on top of the existing text representing the Selected and Activated states. (The Normal layer is still the one embedded into the video footage.)

Once again we will need our frame reference image resized to 720 x 534. This is of particular importance when doing text. If the text isn't created exactly the same way, it will be totally off when you go to author it later.

Using the same text, in this case 18-point Arial Black, retype the same text (Play Movie, Scene Selection, Special Features) as three individual new Layers.

Even though I'm using the chroma method, I've made the text a gray color. The color will be changed later in the process.

I've also added a 3-point black stroke around the text to make sure that it will indeed cover up the text, with no possibility of any of the Normal layer embedded in the footage being seen.

As before, we can now turn off or discard the video reference frame. Now this is where things start to deviate from the prior method. At this point, with only the three [missing word?] Highlight Text selected, you need to flatten the image. All three layers will combine on a solid white background.

Next we want to get rid of all the color information (regardless of the fact that we are only currently using white, black, and a light gray).

Convert the document to Grayscale (Image > Mode > Grayscale). A dialogue box will appear asking you if you want to Discard color information? Click OK to continue.

Now that the color information is deleted you need to convert it back into RGB Mode to work with the chroma colors (Image > Mode > RGB).

The next step requires you to posterize the text into 4 Levels. Choose Posterize (Image > Adjustments > Posterize) and set the Levels to 4. Click OK to continue.

Once again, you will now change the Mode from RGB to Indexed Color (Image > Mode > Indexed Color).

A dialogue box will appear with a number of options. They should remain at their defaults:

> Palette: Exact
>
> Forced: None
>
> Transparency: Unchecked

Click OK to continue.

The last major step in this process is to assign the chroma colors to the four different values of gray. In the Mode pull-down menu, select Color Table (Image > Mode > Color Table). The Color Table dialogue box will appear with the four gray colors represented as squares in the chart.

One at a time, you will need to select each color square and enter the color values in the R, G, and B fields.

For the first square (white), you will need to enter the values for White:

R = 255, G = 255, B = 255.

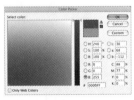

For the second square (light gray), you will need to enter the values for Blue:

R = 0, G = 0, B = 255.

For the third square (dark gray), you will need to enter the values for Red:

R = 255, G = 0, B = 0.

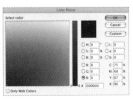

For the fourth square (black), you will need to enter the values for Black:

R = 0, G = 0, B = 0.

When you are done changing the values, you will see that your original black and gray text is now predominantly blue with touches of red and black.

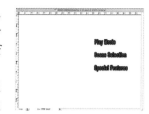

As with the roadside overlay, you now need to resize the document to match the encoded video track. Choose Image Size (Image > Image Size) and resize it to 720 x 480.

Instead of saving the file as a Photoshop (.psd) file, save it as a TIFF (.tif).

From the File pull-down menu select Save As. In the Save As dialogue box choose TIFF under Format.

The TIFF Options dialogue box will appear. Under Image Compression select None and in the Byte Order section choose what type of computer you will be authoring on. DVD Studio Pro is a Macintosh-based program, so that is the one I will select. Click OK to save the finished file.

You've got Menus.

▸ STEP 7: PREPARATION OF SLIDESHOWS

Using still pictures and text in your DVD project not only adds extra production value, it can also be a valuable promotional tool. Consider these possibilities that can be added with very little effort:

- ▸ Cast & Crew Biographies
- ▸ Production Notes
- ▸ Website Information
- ▸ Trivia Test
- ▸ Conceptual Art
- ▸ Storyboards
- ▸ Publicity Stills
- ▸ Poster Art
- ▸ DVD Credits

Most of the assets required to make these useable in your DVD project are probably already filed away on your hard drive or are on hand for scanning. Another advantage is that they take up relatively little space on the disc.

You could choose to do any of these as a Menu with buttons, or you could create a Stills Gallery (or Slideshow). Like its real-world counterpart, a DVD Slideshow is a series of pictures and/or graphics displayed in a linear order. When the DVD is multiplexed, the series is turned into a track with each slide represented as a different track. This means that, as with video tracks, you are limited to 99 slides.

One major advantage to using Slideshows is that it saves a tremendous amount of time in the authoring. Given recent technical advances, you have many different options at your fingertips that will greatly enhance their presentation. You can control the length of time a slide stays on screen (from one second to eight) as well as add music to the background which can be synchronized with the slides (or not, if you prefer).

Before we get into the nuts and bolts of creating a Slideshow, we should take a step back and discuss how the assets are developed.

FORMATS

DVD Studio Pro accepts a wide variety of formats that pretty much encompass every graphic program on the market:
> Adobe Photoshop PSD files (8-bit RGB mode)
> PICT format files
> BMP format files
> JPEG format files
> Quick Time image files
> Targa (TGA) format files
> TIFF (TIF) format files

TEXT

You could have the most gorgeous Cast & Crew Bios known to man, superbly written and surrounded by inspired artwork, but if you can't read them because the text is either too small or too blurry then what's the point. As we mentioned with menus, using an 18-point sans-serif font is recommended.

Real-Life Example — I had an experience somewhat like this for a DVD I authored for the feature *Getting Out of Rhode Island*. This clever experimental film, shot in one night in 2001 and directed by Christian de Rezendes, tells the story of how a man returns to his hometown in Rhode Island and comes to some realizations about life and friendship at a welcome-home party in his honor.

They decided that they wanted to have a Cast & Crew Biography section that would be done as a Stills Gallery. At first glance, everything they sent me seems fine. The format is correct, everything is in TV safe, and it has a nice look that goes well with the flavor of the rest of the menus. The problem is that the text is small, even on a computer screen, let alone somebody's portable handheld DVD player. That's right folks, considering that many people can now watch and enjoy your product on a small handheld device or on a small screen in a car, you should keep them in mind when you are creating your content.

The solution to this problem was simple: Create two screens instead of one.

CREATING STILL IMAGES

This process is similar in many ways to creating layered Photoshop menus. Once again you start by launching Adobe Photoshop.

From the File drop-down menu select New. A dialogue box will appear.

Click on the Preset Sizes drop-down menu and select 720 x 534 Std. NTSC DV/DVD.

A dialogue box will appear. Type in a name in the Name Field. We will call it "GALLERY-Picture(1-18)." Finally, make sure the Mode is set for RGB Color. Click OK to continue.

You will now have a blank canvas to work with.

I decided to use the same type of map we used for our Cast & Crew Bios as the background for out Stills. But this time I only dropped the opacity to 85%.

At this point you should make sure that everything is in the TV Title Safe area. Use the Guides we created in the menu chapter by locating the file and cutting and pasting the Guides layer into this new document.

If you need to recreate them, start by making sure that the measurements are set to percent by selecting Unit & Rulers (Preferences > Units & Rulers). In the Units & Rulers dialogue box, use the Rulers pull-down menu in the Units section to change the measurements to percent. Make sure that the Rulers are visible (View > Rulers) and using the Move tool, drag Guides (top, bottom, left, and right) into the 5% areas for Action Safe and 10% areas for Title Safe. Creating a Menu 720 x 534, the NTSC Title Safe areas are 72 pixels in on the left and right sides and 54 pixels in on the top and bottom. Use Ruler Guides to set these parameters.

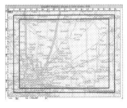

Next you want to add in your picture. I chose a picture of two of the actors in wardrobe between takes. Considering that the McCohen Brothers play an important part in our main character's journey, I thought it might be appropriate to have a candid shot of the two actors who play them. Having imported the picture, I sized it to fit in the center of the frame, leaving

room above and below for text and a little breathing room on the side. I also added a black frame and a drop shadow to make it stand out from the background.

You could stop there and be done with it, but I think it's good form to add some text so the viewers know what they're looking at. At the very least put a counter somewhere on the page (e.g. 1 of 18). I do this because there are so many DVDs that appear to have an endless stream of pictures. If the viewer knows what they're in for, they are more likely to take the journey than to press the Menu button on the remote before the presentation is finished.

Slideshow Etiquette — I would propose that 25 slides in a gallery is more than enough. A longer show may bore your viewer. If you have a large number of pictures that you want to present, I suggest having more than one Slideshow. For example, you might have a slideshow for production art, another for behind-the-scenes pictures, and a third for posters and publicity material. Not only is this more enjoyable for the viewer but it also gives them the impression that they are getting more on the disc. Remember Value-Added Content?

I added the picture counter at the top: (1 of 18) and a description of the picture at the bottom: On the set with the McCohen Brothers (Jason Goldberg & Barry Fine). I used an unsaturated blue text and added a black stroke and a 2-point outline for both.

Now that we are done with the first Slide, I highly recommend saving the unflattened document as a separate .psd file using the Save As option in the File pull-down menu (File > Save as). Call it GALLERY-Template. This way you can create the rest of your slides quite easily by swapping out the pictures and the text and saving them as their own files. This will save you an enormous amount of time because you won't have to start from scratch every time.

FLATTEN IMAGE

The next thing that you want to do is combine all four layers into one using the "Flatten" function. To do this, first turn off the Guides layer. Then choose Flatten Layers from the Layers pull-down menu (Layers > Flatten Layers). A dialogue box will appear asking you if you want to Discard hidden layers? Select OK to continue. The combined layers will automatically be named Background.

RESIZE THE IMAGE

We now need to resize the image to the correct proportions so that it can be imported into the authoring software. Recall that we began with the size 720 x 534. We now want to resize it to 720 x 480. Do this by selecting Image Size from the Image pull-down menu (Image > Image Size).

A dialogue box will appear. Uncheck the Constrain Properties box (if it's checked) and then type in 480 in the Height Field where it currently says 534.

Click OK to continue.

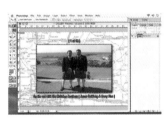

SAVE AS A PICT FILE

Finally, the last step is to save your completed picture as a PICT File (.pct). As I mentioned before, DVD Studio Pro will accept many different formats. I prefer the PICT format and will use it for my demonstration.

First choose Save As from the File pull-down menu (File > Save As).

The Save As dialogue box will appear. Using the Format pull-down menu, choose PICT File (Format > PICT File).

The PICT File Options dialogue box will appear. In the Resolution section select "32 bits/pixel" and in the Compression section select None.

Click OK to save the graphic file. Repeat this process for all your Slideshow images.

INSTRUCTION PAGE

Because there are different ways to author DVDs, it can sometimes be confusing for the viewer to know how to skip through the Stills Gallery pictures or return to the previous menu. Even if you give each picture a certain time limit, some people like to view them at their own (faster) pace or they might just want to skip ahead to a different section of your Gallery.

I find that you can eliminate confusion by making an Instruction Page that appears before the Stills Gallery pictures. In essence it's just another slide with a text message as opposed to a picture. It's made exactly the same way as before and when you author the Slideshow, you place it first in the series.

I use the text: "Use the >>| button on your remote to browse through the Stranded gallery. Press Menu to return to the Special Features Menu."

SLIDESHOW EXAMPLES

As I mentioned before, there are many types of possible Slideshows. Here are some other examples:

We're almost there: just one more step to think about.

▸ STEP 8: SUBTITLES

Let's say that you want your DVD project to be enjoyed by more than just the English-speaking populace of the world. As we've mentioned before, there are many non-English speaking countries that utilize the NTSC signal. One way to include them is to either dub your movie in a foreign language (really expensive and time-consuming) or provide a text translation of your dialogue that appears at the bottom of the screen. These are known as subtitles and you've probably seen them every time you've watched a foreign film yourself.

DVD-Video specification gives you the ability to have multiple (up to 32) subtitle streams.

If you decide you want to use subtitles in your DVD project, realize that this is a time-consuming project. Unless you can translate your dialogue into other languages, you're going to have to find someone to do it for you. (Subtitles are also discussed in Section V in connection with foreign distribution.)

Real-Life Example — One of the most bizarre DVDs I have had the oppor-tunity to author also happens to be one of my favorites: David and Nathan Zellner's *Frontier*. Based on the surrealistic novel *Froktog* by Mulner Typsthat, it tells the tale of two members of the Expansionist Research Corps who embark on a journey to civilize the most uncharted of territories. A U.S.-Bulbovia co-production, the film was shot entirely in Bulbovia in native Bulbovian... Did I mention that there is no such place as Bulbovia?

Considering that, other than David and Nathan, no one on this planet speaks Bulbovian, they were shrewd enough to want subtitles on their DVD. But English subtitles was just not enough for these "zany" brothers. They also wanted French, Spanish, and, get this, Esperanto, for a total of four subtitle streams. This is nowhere near the 32 subtitle streams that are available to use, but nonetheless it does create a challenge.

There are two ways to create subtitles. One way allows you to type them in one at a time directly into DVD Studio Pro (which has greatly improved this method in Version 2, but is still a rather tedious process). The other permits you to create them in an outside text program and import them later.

For the purpose of this book we will discuss the importable version. This method is worth knowing because it allows you to create all your sub-title streams at once and fully control how they will appear in your final DVD project. It is also far less time-consuming and allows you to use the text program's spell-check to search for errors.

Subtitle streams have a wide variety of uses. Not only can they display text (such as dialogue or production information), they can also display graphics that can be used to either enhance the video or as Interactive Markers (buttons that appear within the video). They also can be used for Closed Captions for the hearing-impaired.

Closed Captions — There is a difference between subtitles and closed cap-tions. Subtitles are generally used to display the dialogue of a movie in a different language but assumes that the viewer can hear the original audio. Closed captions, on the other hand, are specifically designed for hearing-impaired individuals and contain sound descriptions as well as dialogue (for example, if there is gunfire the caption reads "Gunshots fired" or if a phone rings, "Ring Ring").

This method also requires the use of a decoder (either a stand-alone unit or one incorporated into a TV) for playback which is typically not included on home computers. This format also limits your ability to control the text (the closed caption decoder chooses the font). In addition, closed captions supported by the DVD specification apply to NTSC programs only.

CREATING IMPORTABLE SUBTITLES

There are some pretty stiff rules that you must follow to have your subtitle file import correctly but new advances with DVD Studio Pro 2 now allow you to import a wide variety of industry standard formats:

- SCR — Scenarist bitmap-based format
- SON — Sonic Solutions bitmap-based format
- STL — Spruce Technologies subtitle format
- TXT — Plain text file

The STL format is the most popular and is rather easy to master, especially if you've had any experience with HTML or scripting.

There are two different ways of importing files into DVD Studio Pro: Single Subtitle Files and Group of Graphics Files.

SINGLE SUBTITLE FILES

The first is the Single Subtitle File. This method must contain three very important pieces of information separated by commas:

- In timecode value
- Out timecode value
- Subtitle text

What follows is an example of a Single Subtitle file:

00:00:09:08, 00:00:12:17, Making Subtitles is fun and easy
00:00:13:02, 00:00:18:21, You can learn it in just minutes

00:00:20:07, 00:00:25:07, Just follow the instructions…
00:00:27:09, 00:00:31:19, And nobody gets hurt.
00:00:32:02, 00:00:37:29, I think you get the point

Your subtitles can be as long as you like, provided that they don't cross a chapter marker or a track. Keep in mind that if the subtitle is the length of the entire track, then changing subtitle streams while you are watching the DVD in mid-track is physically impossible. This is because in order to switch subtitle streams the current subtitle clip must come to an end and then a new clip has to begin. If the stream never terminates, than you are prevented from every changing it.

You can also use simple commands to apply color, alignment, fade in and fade out as well as a variety of styles to your subtitle text. The only disadvantages to using this type of subtitle method is that you must have the correct fonts installed in your authoring system and you are limited to only using text as opposed to graphics.

GROUP OF GRAPHICS FILES

This method allows you to use a graphic file to be your subtitle clip, which means you are not limited to just using text. Like the Single Subtitle methods it must contain three pieces of information.

- ▸ In timecode value
- ▸ Out timecode value
- ▸ Graphic file

What follows is an example of a Group of Graphics file:

$SetFilePathToken = <<Graphic>>
00:00:09:08, 00:00:12:17, <<Graphic>>Nevada#1.tiff
00:00:13:02, 00:00:18:21, <<Graphic>>Nevada#2.tiff
00:00:20:07, 00:00:25:07, <<Graphic>>Soda Can.tiff

Notice that you have to use the $SetFilePathToken command in the file before any line that uses a Graphic File. The graphic files must also be located in the same folder as the subtitle file and cannot be moved, renamed, or deleted once you've begun the authoring process.

With the STL format you have the ability to mix and match between the Single Subtitle files and the Group of Graphics files, provided that you follow the Control Commands.

CONTROL COMMANDS

As mentioned before, DVD Studio Pro will recognize control commands that will override and preset subtitle preferences. Below is a series of commands that you can use to create various methods of presenting your subtitle text.

Text Commands

$FontName: Sets the font by choosing its family name ($FontName = Arial)

$FontSize: Sets the size of the font ($FontSize = 14)

$Bold: True equals Bold version, False equals regular version ($Bold = True)

$Italic: True equals italicized version, False equals regular version ($Italic = True)

$Underlined: True equals underlined, False equals not underlined ($Underlined = True)

Color Commands

Use these commands to select a value between 0 and 15. These colors can be preset in DVD Studio Pro (Preferences > Color Palette).

$ColorIndex1: Text Color ($ColorIndex1 = 1)

$ColorIndex2: Text Outline 1 color ($ColorIndex2 = 1)

$ColorIndex3: Text Outline 2 color ($ColorIndex3 = 1)

$ColorIndex4: Background Color Opacity ($ColorIndex4 = 0)

Contrast Commands

Use these commands to set the opacity of the text by using a value between 0 and 15. 0 = transparent, 15 = opaque.

$TextContrast: Text Color Opacity ($TextContrast = 15)

$Outline1Contrast: Text Outline 1 Color Opacity ($Outline 1Contrast = 15)

$Outline2Contrast: Text Outline 2 Color Opacity ($Outline2Contrast = 15)
$BackgroundContrast: Background Color Opacity
($BackgroundContrast = 0)

Position Commands
Use these command to set the alignment of the text.

$HorzAlign: Left, Right or Center ($HorzAlign = center)
$VertAlign: Top, Bottom or Center ($VertAlign = bottom)
$XOffset: Positive pixel values shifts horizontal alignment to the
Right. Negative pixel values shifts horizontal alignment to the Left
($XOffset = -24)
$YOffset: Positive pixel values shifts vertical alignment Up. Negative
pixel values shifts vertical alignment Down ($YOffset = 34)

Display Commands
$ForceDisplay: Used to force the display of subtitles whether they are
turned on or off. True forces the display, False leaves the control up to
the viewer. ($ForceDisplay = True)
$FadeIn: Sets Fade In time in frames ($FadeIn = 30)
$FadeOut: Sets Fade Out time in frames ($FadeOut = 30)

Timeline Commands
$TapeOffset: Used to reference which timecode is used. True uses the
stream's zero-based timecode, False uses the asset-based timecode.
($TapeOffset = True).

EMBEDDED CONTROL COMMANDS

Another method is to use commands that are embedded within the subtitle text.

Embedded Line Break Command
If a subtitle needs to be spread over two or more lines, you can add a line
break using a vertical pipe character (|).

00:00:13:02, 00:00:18:21, Two lines can sometimes | be better than one.

Embedded Text Commands

Like the regular commands, these will alter the look of the text.

Bold: use ^B

00:00:13:02, 00:00:18:21, Bold ^Btext^B makes things stand out.

Italic: use ^I

00:00:20:07, 00:00:25:07, Italicized ^Iwords^I can attract the eye.

Underline: use ^U

00:00:27:09, 00:00:31:19, Underline important ^Uwords^U in your text.

SAVING SUBTITLE FILES

Once you have finished your subtitle file, simply save it as a TXT file (.txt) and it is ready to import.

With all our assets organized and prepared, we're finally ready to actually author the DVD.

Section 4 AUTHORING THE DVD

We've identified and organized our assets. Now we're ready to create, or "author," the DVD itself.

In this section, we will create, test, burn, and manufacture the DVD. Once again we will use our fictitious DVD project *Stranded* as a model. And once again, the process can be broken down into a series of steps.

STEP 1: IMPORTING ASSETS

STEP 2: AUTHORING MENUS

STEP 3: AUTHORING TRACKS

STEP 4: AUTHORING SLIDESHOWS

STEP 5: LINKING ASSETS

STEP 6: TESTING

STEP 7: MANUFACTURING

By the end of this section, you should have a clear understanding of how a DVD project is authored and ultimately manufactured for distribution.

▸ STEP 1: IMPORTING ASSETS

This is the moment you've been waiting for: authoring. Yeah!

There are many authoring software programs available (and not enough room in this book to teach you each one), so we need to choose one. The most popular authoring programs on the market today are Sonic Scenarist, Creator Fusion, and Apple DVD Studio Pro.

All of these are excellent programs and there are people who swear by each of them for one reason or another. But like in *Sophie's Choice*, I can only pick one.

For me, it's Apple DVD Studio Pro. Not only is this an extremely user-friendly program, it's also very inexpensive. At about $500, DVD Studio Pro 3 is truly a bargain, especially compared to Sonic Scenarist and Sonic Creator, both of which have a price tag in the over-$20,000 range.

This book is not meant as an endorsement of DVD Studio Pro 3. That happens to be the software that I feel will best teach you the basics of DVD authoring, which you can then apply to other programs as well. This book is not meant to be a DVD Studio Pro 3 manual either. For more specific information or advanced techniques relating to particular software, I suggest consulting a user's manual.

Our first step, again, is to take a look at our assets and make sure that they are all where they should be. In the last section we learned how to create different types of assets and save them into pre-made folders. Let's review these folders and see how they should look now.

Every asset related to your DVD project should be stored in the STRANDED DVD folder. For now we will only be dealing with the Menus, Slideshow, and Tracks folders.

MENUS FOLDER

This folder should contain all four of our menus: Cast & Crew Bios, Main, Scene Selection, and Special Features.

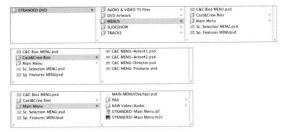

Because the Main Menu has a video, audio, and overlay file, it has been given its own folder. The individual Cast & Crew sub-menus are also contained in a separate folder.

SLIDESHOW FOLDER

This folder should contain all the Stills Gallery pictures.

TRACKS FOLDER

This folder should contain all the video files to be used in the DVD: Behind-the-Scenes Featurette, Main Feature, and Trailer. Each one of these folders will contain the MPEG-2 files that you encoded as well as the AC-3 Files.

There are new sub-folders in each folder called RAW Video/Audio. These are to store the original QuickTime Movies and AIFF Sound Files. It's worth holding onto these in case you need to re-encode because of space or defect issues.

The PAR folder is created by DVD Studio Pro and contains information necessary to import the files. If they are not present at this time, they will be automatically created when the files are imported into the program.

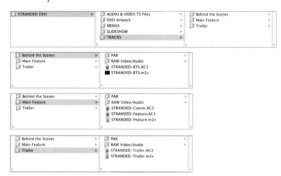

LAUNCHING DVD STUDIO PRO

We are now ready to begin authoring the DVD, so start by launching DVD Studio Pro.

As mentioned before, we are using DVD Studio Pro 3, which has a more advanced interface than its earlier incarnations, especially versions 1 and 1.5.

The program has three different interface configurations: Basic, Extended, and Advanced. Basic is used if you plan to utilize the templates and styles provided by DVD Studio Pro, Extended offers you more control, and Advanced gives you access to all the program's capabilities.

Even though we will only be scratching the surface of what this program can accomplish, we will use the Advanced configuration. This will also make the information more relevant for those who choose to author on another program.

Interface Overview — It's worth pointing out the six different areas of the Advanced interface so you can get a better sense of how a DVD is put together. We'll work our way around the interface in a clockwise manner.

In the upper left corner are the Outline and Graphical Tabs. The Outline Tab lists all the elements in your DVD Project divided by type. Think of it as file folders that you use on your desktop. The Graphical Tab (which was absent from version 2) contains a tile-based view of your project. Similar to the flowchart you created, this is extremely helpful for getting a complete overview of how all your elements connect to one another. It can also be printed out and compared to your original flowchart.

Even though the Graphical Tab is an extremely useful tool for creating your DVD, I will focus more on the use of the Outline Tab for those that are still using DVD Studio Pro 2. I do however highly recommend upgrading to version 3 at some point because of the re-inclusion of the Graphical interface. Not only is it more intuitive, but it has many similarities to other, higher-priced DVD software programs, especially Sonic Scenarist and Creator.

In the upper center are the Menu, Viewer and Connection Tabs. The Menu Tab contains the Menu Editor which displays all the selected menu's content and allows you to configure the buttons. The Viewer Tab allows you to watch the individual video elements and is used for editing subtitles. The Connection Tab is an all-encompassing way to link elements and is necessary for some advanced functions.

In the upper right corner is the Templates Palette which contains pre-made menus, styles, and buttons and allows you to store your own (as well as audio, video and still files) for future projects. Storing in this palette does not import files into your project; it is only a storage filing system.

In the lower right is the Property Inspector. Depending on what element is selected, this palette will give you access to various controls and advanced settings.

In the lower center are the Track, Slideshow, Story, and Script Tabs. The Track Tab contains the Track Editor which displays all the video, audio, and subtitle information of the selected track. It's presented as a linear timeline and allows you to edit the tracks and add chapter markers.

The Slideshow Tab contains the Slideshow Editor, which allows you to organize your Stills Galleries and set certain functions and advanced settings.

The Story Tab contains the Story Editor, which allows you to use the chapter markers to rearrange the presentation of your material.

The Script Tab contains the Script Editor, which allows you to set commands to further create advanced navigations and unique presentations.

In the lower left are the Assets and Log Tabs. Perhaps the most important area of the interface, the Assets Tab is where you store all your files for the project so they can be accessed to create the DVD. The Log Tab gives you status information for your DVD Build, Encode, and Simulation.

CREATING A NEW PROJECT

DVD Studio Pro will automatically create a new file for you to work on. If there is currently an active file, simply select New from the File pull-down menu.

There are a number of things that you need to configure before you start importing your assets. You could wait to configure some of them later, but I don't recommend it. Getting in the habit of configuring your new project immediately will save you heartache at the end when you realize, after all the complex stuff you've done, that you completely forgot the basic necessary settings.

The first step is to save your new project. Yep, before you do anything else, save it. And get in the habit of saving it. Often. God forbid that your computer should crash or you have a blackout in the middle of authoring and you haven't saved in awhile. There are so many things to keep track of in so many palettes that forgetting to re-do one of them could completely screw your project.

Select Save from the File pull-down menu and name the DVD Project (STRANDED DVD) and choose a location (STRANDED DVD Folder)

So far, so good.

Let's discuss the areas that you should configure before we really get going. Make sure that STRANDED DVD is selected in the Outline tab and the Property Inspector reads Disc at the top.

In the Disc Inspector you should immediately notice three things. First, the name field contains the name of our DVD Project (STRANDED DVD). Second, even though technically nothing has yet been imported into our DVD, it is already estimated as 113KB in size. Third, the First Play field has

Menu 1 selected. First Play refers to the first thing that appears when the DVD is placed in the player. You can set this to any element in your project.

The default is Menu 1 which means that if you somehow forgot to set this incredibly important function, your disc would still play if you burned it. If it is not set, then the DVD will spin in the player until the cows come home. (For you city folks, that means indefinitely.)

Other than the Name and First Play fields, the General tab contains one other vital setting: Video Standard. Here is where you decide whether the DVD is NTSC or PAL. Choose NTSC for *Stranded*.

In the Disc/Volumes Tab you need to select the Disc Media, Layer Options, Number of Sides, and Disc Size. These do not necessarily need to be determined at this point, but if you know that you're doing a single-layer DVD you might as well set them now. For *Stranded* you will choose 4.7 gigabytes (DVD-5), Single Layer, One Side and we'll be using a 12 cm Disc.

The Region/Copyright Tab allows you to choose in which areas around the world you would like the DVD to be playable. One must be selected. There is no reason to uncheck any of them unless you plan to release different versions in the various regions. Why limit the potential viewership of your DVD? Just because a region may be PAL does not mean that they don't have the ability to watch an NTSC DVD.

Copyright Management allows you to set copy protection options. You must first select No Copy Permitted to access either CSS (Content Scrambling System), which prevents digital copying, or Macrovision, which prevents analog duplication.

Macrovision is a proprietary product and you must enter a usage agreement with Macrovision Corp. before you can officially use it. For more information visit www.macrovision.com.

We will leave the Copyright section untouched. Activating these settings can affect your ability to duplicate and/or replicate your finished project. So unless you are planning to make only one copy, leave these controls alone.

The Advanced tab contains specialized features that need to be preset if you choose to use them. The Embedded Text Data allows the DVD player to display the names of tracks, menus, and slideshows on the screen as you watch the movie. (You must use the display button on your DVD player remote control to access this.) You will need to choose the language of the text as well.

The Additional Remote Controls section allows you to override defaults and set your own links. There is no reason to touch these for our project. Besides, the default settings have been chosen for a reason.

The GPRM Variable Names is an advanced scripting feature so we will not be dealing with it. For more information on scripting you should consult the user's manual for your authoring program.

IMPORTING THE ASSETS: PART I

There is one more thing I like to do before I start importing the elements. The Assets Tab allows you to create folders to better manage the assets. Keep in mind that even a small DVD project has many elements, and trying to keep track of them all can get confusing. So making folders similar to the ones we've made before can really save you a lot of frustration in the long run.

Using the New Folder button (located on the Palette), create three folders and label them: MENUS, SLIDESHOWS, and TRACKS.

We are now ready to import our DVD Assets. There are three ways of doing this. Use either the Import button on the palette or the Import Asset icon on the toolbar. Both of these will import directly into the Assets Tab.

Another method allows you to drag and drop from an open folder directly into the Assets Tab. This is a handy method to use because not only is it fast, but you can grab multiple items at once and easily keep track of what you've imported.

The third method allows you to drag and drop your files directly into the project elements. DVD Studio Pro will automatically add the imported asset in the Assets Tab.

Start with the menus. Drag and drop all the menus, including the Cast & Crew Bios and the Main Menu files, directly into the MENU Folder.

Next, drag and drop all the Stills Gallery pictures, including the Stills Gallery Instructions, into the SLIDESHOW Folder.

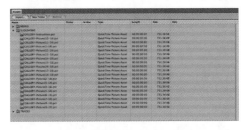

Finally, drag and drop all the Tracks into the TRACKS Folder. There should be one video file (.m2v) and one audio file (.AC3) for each

(except for the Main Feature which will have two audio files).

Parse Files — There is certain information that DVD Studio Pro needs about your assets. This information is contained in what is known as a Parse File (.par). Depending on how you encoded the files, a parse file was either created or not. Some encoders require you to choose the option while others do it automatically. If for some reason a parse file does not exist, DVD Studio Pro will make one for you when you import the file into the Assets Tab. Depending on the size of the element, this can take anywhere from several seconds to a few minutes. This happens in the background and the file will be unavailable for use until the parse file is created.

You will notice that the Assets Tab contains important information about your files including File Type, Length, Size, and Bit Rate. This can be very valuable information if you find that your DVD is packed to the gills and you need to eliminate files or have files that you might want to re-encode in order to reduce their size. The In Use column is currently empty, but as we start assigning these Assets to various functions, this will keep track of them for you, making it easy to see at the end of authoring if you've forgotten something or not.

Non-DVD Compliant Files — If any of the files are rejected while trying to import them, it means that something was done incorrectly in the preparation. You need to evaluate each rejected element on a file-to-file basis and review the steps to see where you might have made a mistake. I highly suggest dealing with these problems and solving them before you continue the authoring process. It is best to only create a DVD when you have all the assets imported successfully into your DVD project. Piece-mealing a project together can cause confusion and the loss of necessary assets if you aren't careful.

IMPORTING THE ASSETS: PART 2

Now that we have imported all the elements into DVD Studio Pro, we need to utilize them in the project itself. Remember, the Assets Tab is just a storage space for aliases of your files. At this point you've only done half the job of actually importing them. Here's how the other half is done.

We'll start with the menus.

Using the elements in the Assets Tab as a reminder guide, I will create menus in the Outline Tab. The easiest way to do this to use the tools in the toolbar.

Add Menu refers to any type of standard highlight menu whether it be Motion or Static. Add Layered menu refers to any menu that uses a Layered file for its button states (for example, Layered Photoshop file).

Our DVD project has seven standard menus (the three menus and four bios menus) and one layered menu (the Scene Selection menu). Using the Toolbar, add six more standard menus (one is automatically created when you start a new project) with the Add Menu button and one layered menu with the Add Layered Menu button.

Rename them to correspond with the Menus we want: Main Menu, Scene Selection Menu, Special Features Menu, Cast & Crew Bios Menu, Director Bio, Producer Bio, Actor #1 Bio and Actor #2 Bio.

Make sure that you name the layered menu "Sc. Selection Menu." It has to be put in that file folder.

Now, one at a time, simply drag and drop the menu file from the Assets Tab into the corresponding file holder in the Outline Tab. For the Main Menu, just drag the .m2v file. For any file that has a separate overlay file (if you chose to do it that way), just drag the Background only. You will assign the Overlay later.

You will notice that in the Menu Viewer the Main Menu (or whatever you assign to Menu 1) will appear.

Using the View pull-down menu in the Menu Viewer you can scroll down all the menus and see whether they imported correctly. If there is nothing there, that means you didn't drag it in successfully. Try again, because at this point the Menu is viable and should be able to import fully with no problems.

We will return to the actual authoring of the menus after we have finished importing the rest of the elements.

Continuing the process, we'll move on to the tracks, which uses a similar process. This time we will need to add only three tracks based on our Assets Tab.

Using the Add Track button in the Toolbar, add two more tracks (as before, one is automatically created when you start a new project) into our project.

There are two time-saving shortcuts to consider. You can create the Track file holders and drag and drop the files from the Assets tab and they will automatically be renamed. To save even more time, you can just drag and drop files from the Assets Tab into the Outline Tab (without adding tracks), and new tracks will be created and named as well. Consult the Studio Pro user's manual for information on other shortcuts and various ways to import elements.

Like before, drag and drop the Track files from the Assets tab into the unnamed track holders in the Outline tab. As long as the audio files have the same name (i.e. STANDED-BTS.m2v and STRANDED-BTS.AC3), DVD Studio Pro knows they are linked and will import them at the same time. If they have different names you will have to manually drag and drop them yourself.

Even though they will already be named, rename them to make them easier to recognize while we author: Feature, Behind the Scenes, Trailer.

You should also notice that in the Timeline your tracks have appeared in the V1 stream with their respective audio tracks listed in the A1 stream.

Because the *Stranded* Feature also has a commentary track (STRANDED-Comm.AC3), that needs to be brought in as well.

The easiest way to do this is to simply drag and drop it directly into the timeline in the A2 stream. This instantly makes it a secondary audio track for the Main Feature.

Our last step in importing the files is to add the Slideshow stills. As you've already guessed, this is done

just like you did the Menus and Tracks. Using the Add Slideshow button in the tool-

bar, create a slideshow (a necessary step because a slideshow is not automatically created when you begin a new project).

Select all the Stills files in the Assets Tab and drag and drop them into the newly created Slideshow holder in the Outline tab. Rename the Slideshow to Stills Gallery to avoid confusion later.

If you select the Slideshow tab in the timeline, you can scroll through the pictures that you've imported. We will discuss the manipulation of the Slideshow Assets later in this section.

Disc Meter — If you look in the toolbar you will see a Disc Meter that lets you know how much space you are using on the DVD at any precise moment. If it's not there, add it to the toolbar using Customize Toolbar (View > Customize Toolbar).

Now that we have imported all our files you can see how much space it takes up. According to the meter, we are using 4.3 GB of space. Considering that we have 4.38 GB and we're not planning to add anything else, it looks like we did our homework well when budgeting this DVD.

At this point you have learned how to import your prepared elements into DVD Studio Pro. The following section deals with the meat and potatoes of DVD authoring: assigning and linking elements.

▶ STEP 2: AUTHORING MENUS

Now that the menus are imported into the DVD project, we can now author them. What we need to accomplish is for each Menu to have working buttons with three different states that do something when you activate them.

There are three steps to follow in order to author the menus:
- ▸ Creation of Buttons
- ▸ Assigning of Button States
- ▸ Linking Elements

Before we get into these, we should first become familiar with the Menu Inspector.

MENU INSPECTOR

In order to access the Menu options in the Property Inspector, select the menu you want to access, either in the Outline Tab or the Viewer pull-down menu. I chose the Main Menu, which is a standard menu (the Menu Inspector will have different options for a layered menu).

At the very top of the Inspector there are three settings: Name, Est. Size, Background. If you haven't already named the menu you can do it here (or change the name). Est. Size tells you approximately how much disc space this particular menu is using. Background lets you choose the main image for the menu. In our case it's a movie file (STRANDED-Main  Menu.m2v). By using the Background pull-down menu, you have access to every available element in the Assets tab.

You will also notice that there are five tabs: General, Menu, Transition, Colors, Advanced. I will briefly discuss some of these options; for more in-depth explanations, consult a user's manual.

We will not discuss the use of Transitions in this book. It is an advanced function found only in DVD Studio Pro 3 and is not relevant to our project. That said, it is an exciting tool that allows you to add flash and pizzazz to your projects and is worth learning. Once again, I suggest consulting a manual for information on using Transitions.

At the top of the General tab, you can control aspects of the video and/or audio. You can set different Start and End points as well as determine where the video will loop. The Duration will automatically reflect any changes you make. If you decide to change it manually it will affect the end time of your video.

The middle section of the tab is an area designed for Timeout and Jump actions. In the At End pull-down menu you can choose from Still, which freezes the menu at the end of its play; Loop, which will utilize the Start, Loop, and End controls; and Timeout, which allows you to choose for the viewer if they do not activate a button within a specified time.

If you decide to use the timeout action you must decide when in seconds (unless you have a video file with a set duration) and where the menu should go when the time is up. The Action pull-down menu allows you to access any element in the Assets tab.

At the bottom you can assign the Overlay that you want to use for this menu. If you are using a PSD file for either the Background or the Overlay you will need to assign the layers as well. You must choose which layers are always shown and which one layer in particular is the Overlay.

For this menu we have a separate overlay (MAIN MENU Overlay.psd) and you must select it using the Overlay pull-down menu.

The Menu tab allows for a number of advanced options. The only options that are of real significance are the Aspect Ratio field and the Audio section. You must choose whether the Aspect Ratio of the menu is 4:3 or 16:9. Because *Stranded* is 4:3 all our menus will use that ratio as well.

The Audio field allows you to select an audio file that can be used with the menu if you so desire. Because we gave ours the same name as the menu (STRANDED-Main Menu.aif), DVD Studio Pro automatically imported it for us.

The Colors tab allows you to choose either the Simple or Advanced color settings. (We will discuss Advanced color settings later in this section.)

The Simple settings allow you to create three unique configurations in which you can have different colors representing the Selected and Activated layers. These are assigned in the Button Inspector but can be determined in the Menu Inspector. You can also choose the opacity of the overlay color.

The Advanced tab allows you to control various functions allowed by the remote control. It is broken up into four sections: Playback Control, Stream Selection, Menu Call, and Button.

If you enable any of these selections you block the viewer from being able to control these functions.

The buttons at the bottom allow you to disable or enable all of them quickly. You can still make adjustments from either decision.

I don't feel it is necessary to bar the viewer from using these functions. Unless you have a particular reason, I suggest leaving all of these disabled (i.e. unchecked). The DVD experience should be one of choices left to the viewer, not forced upon them. If you want them to watch the content in a restricted manner then release your project solely on VHS.

CREATING BUTTONS (STANDARD HIGHLIGHT MENUS)

Even though we have created menus with either overlays or layered buttons, the buttons themselves do not exist yet. In this section we will make the button zones that will allow the overlays and the layers to work.

The process is easy. Simply place your cursor anywhere on the actual menu in the Menu Viewer, press the mouse button and drag the cursor. A resizable box will be created (as large as the screen if so desired). It will be automatically be named Button 1 and the Button Inspector will now be accessible.

You need to create a button for each of the menu options (in this case, three), and position them over the pre-made overlay pictures.

The best way to see where the buttons should be positioned is to use the Settings pull-down menu in the upper right corner of the Viewer area and select Display Overlay. It will appear solid white but as you position the buttons the layer will be revealed.

BUTTON INSPECTOR

Like the Menu Inspector, the Button Inspector allows you to choose different options and settings that help better define and author your buttons. At the very top you will find three settings: Name, Button#, Target. The default name for the button is Button 1. It is in your best interest to rename your buttons to correspond with the options they represent. So Button 1 becomes Play Movie, Button 2 becomes Sc. Selection, and Button 3 becomes Sp. Features.

The Button# labels the buttons in the order that they were created. This is important because it is used for Button Hierarchy. Button #1 becomes the default first button. It is possible to control the order of the buttons with advanced features, but if you are just trying to bang out a quick menu, then be aware in what order you create and place them.

The Target pull-down menu is of utmost importance. This choice is at the very heart of authoring. You are deciding where the DVD takes you when this button is activated. The pull-down menu allows you to choose any element in your DVD project. Remember, buttons can lead you anywhere: another menu, a track, a transition video, even back to the same menu. It's totally up to you. For now we will leave them not set. We will discuss the linking of elements later in this chapter.

There are four Tabs associated with the Button Inspector: Style, Advanced, Colors, and Transitions.

Once again, I will be not be discussing the use of Button Transitions at all in this book. Consult a user's manual for information on using these Transitions.

The Style tab allows you to assign an asset as the button, whether it be a picture or a video clip. The other options in the tab control the appearance and functionality of the selected element. We will not be utilizing this method of button design so for more specific information consult a manual.

The Advanced tab has some useful controls. The top area allows you to override the default button navigation. In other words, if you are unhappy with the order of the buttons as you scroll down or you have an odd button configuration that you want better navigational control over, this is where the magic happens.

You can literally decide what button is next, based on which arrow is pressed on the remote control.

This is one of the reasons why it's important to name your buttons. Each arrow position has a pull-down menu that lists all the buttons of the menu you are working on. So having names to choose from is far easier than trying to remember which one is Button 1, 2, 3, and so on.

In the middle of the tab are fields for choosing Angles, Audio, and Subtitle Streams that you might want to assign to a specific button which would override any default streams.

For example, if the button was Director's Commentary (the audio for which is in Stream A2), you could specify the Commentary audio file from the pull-down menu. Then any time this button was chosen it would play the movie with the commentary instead of the original soundtrack.

At the bottom of the tab are controls for manually altering the size of the individual buttons.

The last tab is Colors. This is exactly the same one found in the Menu Inspector and any changes you make in this tab will affect the one in the other.

It's worth talking about the Advanced settings and how we are going to use them for the Main Menu.

By choosing the Advanced option in the Overlay Colors, the appearance of the tab will change, allowing for specific controls. Another important decision is to determine whether this menu will utilize the Chroma or Grayscale mapping method.

As you recall, when we made the Overlay, we used the Chroma method. When selected, the colors in the lower boxes will change from shades of gray to black, red, blue, and white. the exact colors we used to design the overlay.

The Selection State area allows you to specify what each layer will look like. Because Normal is invisible you will not bother with those settings.

You will notice that next to each Chroma color there is a pull-down menu that allows you to choose a color for each one. Next to that is a scroll-bar that sets the color's opacity (between 0 and 15).

Because I want the Selection button states to resemble the real road signs, I've assigned colors to the Chroma to create that. The Chroma black stays black, and the Chroma red is red. The Chroma blue, however, represents what I want to be white, and the Chroma white should be transparent. If the white is not transparent than it will cover up the Background of the menu.

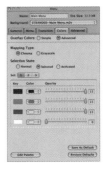

Because I want the road sign overlays to have a very solid feel, the Chroma black, red, and blue should be set to the maximum (which is 15), and because I want the Chroma white to be invisible it should be set for 0 (which is the minimum).

For the activated layers, I decided to be a bit more garish and really emphasize that they were activated.

I wanted all the signs to look neon green with black borders. In order to achieve this, both the Chroma black and red had to be the neon green and the Chroma blue had to be the black. The Chroma white remains at 0 so it stays invisible.

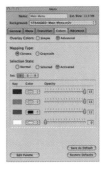

The final effect is rather striking and quite effective. There is no way the viewer will not know they've made their selection.

CREATING BUTTONS (LAYERED MENUS)

Making the buttons for layered menus is the exact same click and drag process, the difference being in how the button layers are dealt with and the variations in the Button Inspector.

The first thing we need to do is select the Scene Selection menu in the Outline tab so we can see it in the viewer. You will notice that all the layers are currently visible. This is because we need to tell DVD Studio Pro which layers we want to always be visible and which layers we want to act as button layers.

You should also notice that the General tab in the Menu Inspector is different from the same tab in the Standard Menu Inspector.

The top section of the tab contains the Timeout settings. Unlike the other menu type, here you only have two options: Still, which will stay on the Menu until an option is activated, and Timeout, which forces a jump action after a determined amount of time when there is no activity. You must choose the amount of time and where the menu will jump to after the time runs out.

The middle section of the tab contains the settings for the background of the menu. The Background pull-down menu allows you to locate the file you want to use from any of your Assets. This will be already filled if you create the menus like we did (importing them directly into the Outline tab). If you just created blank menus, then you would need to select the file first.

Just below is a list of all the layers that comprise your menu and all of them (except the Divider layers) are checked. This is why you can see all the layers. If a box is enabled it means that DVD Studio Pro will always show that layer. Obviously we only want the Background layer to always be visible, so we need to uncheck all the other layers.

It's a good idea to draw your buttons before you disable the Button Layers because with the layers activated, you know precisely where they're supposed to be.

The bottom of the tab contains information regarding any overlays. Because we don't have an overlay file with this menu, you will not need to bother with it.

As I mentioned before, draw all the buttons exactly like you did on the Standard Menu. Place your cursor anywhere on the menu and click and drag to create a box. Because each button is assigned a separate layer, it is not necessary to encapsulate the entire button image, though it is recommended.

Unlike the Highlight method, it is also entirely safe to overlap buttons because they will never be able to incorporate another layer's image unless instructed to do so.

When you create a button, you are in essence creating a "hot zone" or "hot spot." This is important for those viewers who are watching your DVD on a computer. These areas are where they can place the cursor and click to select and activate. It's best to have the button surround the entire text and layer graphic because a big target area means less frustration for the viewer. You want the hot zones obvious, not small and inconvenient to find.

BUTTON INSPECTOR

The Button tab of the Layered Button Property Inspector is almost identical to the Advanced tab in the Standard Button Inspector except for one minor difference. The Button tab contains an area towards the bottom that allows you to choose the Color Mapping Set for your buttons if you choose to use Highlights instead of the layers you created. As before, we will leave the Target as not set for now.

The tab that is the greatest departure from the Standard method is the Layers tab.

Like the Background area in the General tab of the Layered Menu Property Inspector, this tab contains all the layers for the menu. There are also three boxes next to each layer. The first box represents the Normal layer, the second box represents the Selected layer, and the third box represents the Activated layer.

For each individual button you need to assign the layers by enabling the box that corresponds with it.

For example: Button 2 (which we renamed "Dumped") needs to have its three boxes enabled. Because the Background contains the Normal layer, we need to check the first box of the Background layer. The menu's selected layer is labeled 2-Selected. So the second box needs to be checked for the 2-Selected layer. Finally, the menu's activated layer is labeled 2-Activated. So the third box needs to be checked for the 2-Activated layer.

We do not actually need to choose the Background as the Normal layer because it will be displayed by default. But it's a good habit to get into because many times the Normal layer will not be part of the background and you might forget to check it.

The Colors tab is exactly the same as the one for the Standard menus. There is really no reason to use Highlights on a layered menu. You might as well use a Standard menu if you use them, because they operate better when you view the disc.

You should make sure that you rename all the buttons on your menu to correspond with the options they represent. I have taken the opportunity to rename them: Vacation, Dumped, Hitchin', Despair, Realization, Homecoming, Main Menu.

Once again, the reason for doing this is to avoid confusion when you are linking elements, especially when dealing with navigation and returning to a specific button on a menu, which DVD Studio Pro 3 allows you to do.

REPEAT AND SAVE

Now that you have a basic understanding how the buttons are made and the overlays and/or the layers are assigned, repeat this process for all your menus. The only thing that you will not have done when you are finished with this step is linking (Target) the buttons to other menus, tracks, or specific markers. This will be discussed in the Linking section.

Make sure you save, and save often, after each menu you complete. This is a good habit to get into. It's better to save too often than not often enough. It only takes a second or two to hit Command-S. So do it.

▸ STEP 3: AUTHORING TRACKS

In the section on importing assets, we learned how to bring the assets into DVD Studio Pro. Now we need to discuss how they can be modified and ultimately authored.

If you select the Main Feature in the Outline Tab, the viewer will display your movie file, the Track Editor will show the video and sound elements that comprise it, and the Track Inspector will be made available for other modifications. Before we go any further, let's take a closer look at these three areas.

THE VIEWER TAB

The Viewer allows you to preview your tracks with the use of four buttons located at the bottom of the Viewer: Play/Pause, Stop, Skip Forward, and Skip Reverse.

The spacebar on your keyboard can also be used to play and pause the track.

This view window is also used for creating and positioning subtitles.

THE TRACK EDITOR

The Track Editor allows you to manipulate your tracks after they have been imported. This is also where you can set markers to define the different chapters.

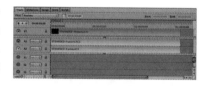

In the upper left corner is the View pull-down menu. Here you can select any of your tracks to work with. Next to it is a timecode counter that identifies the position of the playhead.

Below them are controls that work in the same manner as the Timeline tools in Final Cut Pro. You have the ability to select and lock streams to the left and import assets into the timeline on the right. This gives you the ability to stack video assets one after the other if you want.

The Timeline is broken up into three parallel sections: Video, Audio, and Subtitles. Each track can hold a maximum of nine video streams, eight audio streams, and 32 subtitle streams.

In the upper right corner are two timecode counters labeled Start and End. These will display the position of the first and last frame of a selected clip (video, audio or subtitle). These are useful if you would like to reposition the clip (by altering the Start timecode) or trim it (by altering the End timecode).

THE TRACK INSPECTOR

The Track Inspector consists of four tabs that contain advanced controls for your various video assets.

As with the buttons, I will be not be discussing the use of video transitions. Consult a user's manual for information on using these transitions.

At the very top of the tab are three important settings: Name, Est. Size, and End Jump. Because we imported the video file into the track, the name transfers with it. Feel free to change the name if you desire. Just make sure that it's in some way descriptive of your project.

Est. Size tells you approximately how much space is taken up by the track. This includes any audio and subtitle streams assigned to it.

The End Jump pull-down menu allows you to choose where the DVD will take you once the track has finished. This is one of the most important settings. It must be set or your DVD won't work. When tracks end they usually go back to the menu from which they were accessed or to the main menu (which is typical for the Main Feature).

At the top of the General tab is the Display section where you choose the Mode: either 4:3 or 16:9. Beneath that is the Playback Options section which allows you to choose a predetermined script as well as choose how long the DVD player should wait before it activates the End Jump option. Use the Remote Control section to assign elements if they are activated by the viewer's remote control device.

I tend to set the menu control to the menu from which it was accessed. This makes life easier when you preview the disc and want to instantly return to the previous menu before reaching the end of the track.

The Other tab contains controls for Closed Captions, Timestamps, and Macrovision. For more in-depth explanations of these functions, consult a manual.

The User Operations tab is exactly the same as in all the other Inspectors. Any changes you make are reflected in all the User Operations tabs. As I mentioned before, it's best to leave all the selections disabled (unchecked).

CREATING CHAPTER MARKERS

Markers have a wide variety of uses in your DVD project. Each track can have up to 255 of them and of those, 99 can be used to define chapters. Other uses include defining where the layer break will be on a dual-layered project and identifying places that will be used in advanced scripts.

There are also three different ways to create the markers. You can simply click on the Marker area of the Timeline and drag the automatically created marker to a specified place on the stream, you can import a text file that lists the markers, or you can incorporate markers into your editing timeline before you encode the material.

Pre-placing the markers while editing saves a lot of time during authoring. You must however use Final Cut Pro 3.0.2 (or newer), iMovie 3.0 (or newer), or Final Cut Express. DVD Studio Pro will automatically assign its markers to yours when the file is imported into the timeline.

We've already determined that we have six options (Vacation, Dumped, Hitchin', Despair, Realization, Homecoming) in our *Stranded* DVD Scene Selection menu, so we need to create markers on the timeline of the track to correspond to the beginning timecodes of those chapters.

Because the first chapter is typically the start of the film (as it should be), you do not need to create a marker for it. When you link the Vacation button in the Scene Selection menu, it will simply jump to the start of the track (i.e. Main Feature).

The best place to start is with a list of the specific timecodes that represents the first frame of each chapter. This can either be determined during editing (whether you decide to pre-place markers or not) or after you've imported the file into the timeline. At the very least I suggest you have a vague idea where they should go. The last thing you want to be doing is hunting frame by frame through a 94-minute film searching for reasonable places to set your chapters.

Here are the approximate timecodes for the *Stranded* chapters:

▸ Chapter 1: Vacation   00:00:00;00
▸ Chapter 2: Dumped   00:08:11;19
▸ Chapter 3: Hitchin'   00:30:41;24
▸ Chapter 4: Despair   00:41:31;29
▸ Chapter 5: Realization 01:04:19;26
▸ Chapter 6: Homecoming   01:17:09;11

The simplest way to create these markers in DVD Studio Pro is to click in the Marker area (directly above the Playhead) and a new marker (Chapter 2) will automatically appear. Next, position the playhead on the timeline at the precise timecode by using the Playhead Timecode field and press "M." The marker will be placed directly over the playhead. Repeat this process for the other five chapters.

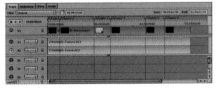

THE MARKER INSPECTOR

The Marker Inspector allows for more specific controls of your markers and is comprised of two tabs: General and User Operations.

At the top of the Marker Inspector are two settings: Name and End Jump. The Name field is where you can assign names to each marker so that they correspond with the chapter names in the Scene Selection menu. This is highly recommended because when we go back and link these to the buttons in the Scene Selection menu, it will be obvious which chapter markers go with which buttons.

Take the time to rename all the markers in the General tabs by selecting each individual marker to access its respective Marker Inspector. The new names will be reflected on the markers in the timeline.

The End Jump setting is only used if you have a specific purpose for a markered section. If not, leave it as not set. If you designate an element for it to jump to, then anytime you reach the end of that marker (no matter how it's accessed), it will jump to the assigned element. By leaving it not set, the track will automatically continue to the next chapter. It goes without saying that this is what you want if your track is your Main Feature.

In the Marker Functions section of the General tab, a thumbnail of the precise frame where the selected marker begins is displayed. Even though it's tiny and can be a pain to use, this is an invaluable tool for making sure that your marker is indeed in the right place.

Most DVD producers try to place chapter markers in between scenes, especially during a fade to black. If this is the case with your movie, then you know the marker is in the right place if the thumbnail is black. If there is an image, however, you need to reposition the marker a couple of frames before or after (depending on where you placed it).

To the immediate left of the thumbnail are Zero-Based and Asset-Based timecodes with up and down arrows that allow you to manually move the marker on the timeline without having to drag it. This gives you near-frame accuracy (based on GOP boundaries).

The middle section of the tab has controls for Playback Options and DVD@ccess. For more information on DVD@ccess, please consult a manual.

As explained before, the User Operations tab contains the same controls as all the other Property Inspector tabs.

REPEAT AND SAVE

Now that you have a basic understanding how the markers are made, repeat this process for any other tracks that require it.

When you are finished with this step, the only thing you will not have done is linking (End Jump) the tracks to other menus, tracks, or specific markers. This will be discussed in the Linking Assets section.

Make sure you save (Command-S) before continuing.

▸ STEP 4: AUTHORING SLIDESHOWS

In the chapter on importing assets we learned how to create a slideshow and import the pictures. We will now discuss how to manipulate these imported elements.

As mentioned before, slideshows can add a lot to your DVD presentation. DVD Studio Pro gives you an array of controls that allow you to tailor the slideshow to your specific needs. You can control the length of each slide and add audio to each individual slide or to the entire slideshow. You can also convert the slide to a track so you can manipulate it even more.

THE SLIDESHOW EDITOR

The main slideshow workspace is the Slideshow Editor. This contains all the slides (pictures) you have imported and the controls for manipulating the presentation. The workspace is split into seven columns: No., Image, File, Audio, Time, Duration, and Pause.

You will immediately notice that a duration of five seconds has already been assigned to each slide. This is typically a comfortable amount of time for an image to appear on the screen. You are by no means locked into this. Slide duration can vary from one second to as long as eight. If you want all of your slides to show at a different, but consistent, duration, then I suggest changing the default length in the General Tab under Preferences (File > Preferences) *before* you import the images. This is worth doing because if you have a large number of slides, individually changing the duration can be a real drag.

The first thing that you want to do is to make sure that the slides are in the proper order. The order is determined from top to bottom. This is why it's a good idea to label your slides by number beforehand.

If necessary, it's very easy to rearrange your slides. Simply select a slide and with the mouse button still depressed, drag it up or downwards and place it between the slides you want. You can also grab multiple slides either by selecting adjacent ones (using the Shift key) or by selecting non-adjacent ones (using the Command key).

By choosing the Pause box next to each slide you are requiring the viewer to manually advance the individual slide during the presentation. Do not, however, use a pause in the last slide. This can affect the ability of some DVD players to enable the End Jump setting and the disc may lock up at the end of your slideshow. Always leave it unchecked.

This is why we created an instruction page. Because there are many different ways to author a slideshow that will ultimately appear the same way when viewed, it can sometimes be hard for the viewer to know what they need to do in order to toggle through the pictures. Considering that you can always skip forward or backward (even if you have durations on your slides), it's best to let the viewer know how. Some people get impatient or just want to see a certain section of your presentation and there is no reason why they should be forced to view the entire sequence.

THE SLIDESHOW CONTROLS

At the top of the Slideshow Editor are various control

settings that deal with adding audio to your slideshow and with the duration of the slides.

If you want audio in the background (either music or descriptive audio), then it needs to be imported into the slideshow. You have a number of options. You can bring in a piece of music and have the slideshow match the length of the audio file, or you can have it loop in the background until the slide presentation is completed. You can also bring in separate audio files and assign them to each individual slide (provided that each audio file is created in the same manner with the same bit rate and resolution).

To use an overall audio file, select the file from your Assets tab and drag and drop it into the Audio Well field.

By using the Settings pull-down menu, you have the ability to decide whether the slides will fit to the audio (the durations will automatically be recalculated) or the audio will fit to the slides (the durations are left untouched). You also have the ability to fit to the slides and loop the audio.

If you choose to fit to slides and the slides finish before the audio, the last slide will remain on the screen until the audio ends. If the audio finishes before the slides then the slides will continue in silence. That is, unless you enable the Loop Audio box which will restart the audio until the last slide is reached and then it will be cut off.

If you want each slide to have its own individual audio file (especially useful for descriptive audio), then you need to import the audio files into the slideshow one at a time. Select the file from the Assets tab and drag it over to the slide in the Slideshow Editor. Release the mouse button and it will be applied to the slide and the duration will change to match the file size. Keep in mind that if you do this you will no longer have the ability to alter the duration.

You also have the ability to choose *Manual Advance*. This negates the slide durations and lets the viewer decide when to advance to the next slide by using the Next button on the remote or by hitting the Play button.

CONVERT TO TRACK

The Slideshow Editor also gives you the option of converting your slideshow into a track. This allows you to add things to your presentation that can't normally be achieved through the Slideshow Editor. For example, you can add multiple audio streams, add subtitles, and combine moving video with the still images.

It is best to make a duplicate of your slideshow before you convert it. Once turned into a track you cannot turn it back. To transform it, make sure it is in the Slideshow Editor and all your settings are correct. Press the Convert To Track button and it will be created. The original slideshow will be deleted (thus the reason you created a back-up).

The track will have markers between all the slides (named for each of the corresponding files). The track will also contain all the audio and any pauses you added.

You will also need to convert to a track if you want to use 16:9 images.

16:9 SLIDESHOWS

You cannot make a 16:9 slideshow presentation unless you first convert it to a track. (The slideshow feature is designed solely for 4:3 images.) Import the 16:9 images into the Slideshow Editor. (Use only 16:9 images; 4:3 will look distorted when they are shown.) Then, after making a duplicate file for safe keeping, press the Convert To Track button.

Finally, in the General tab of the Track Inspector you must select 16:9 for the Aspect Ratio setting.

THE SLIDESHOW INSPECTOR

The Slideshow Inspector has three tabs: General, Advanced, and Transition. The top of this Inspector is the same as the Track Inspector, allowing for Name and End Jump controls.

In the General tab you can only configure the slideshow for overall audio. This allows you to utilize more than one audio file if you want. This will be negated if you either choose to add audio to the individual slides or if you use no audio at all.

THE SLIDE INSPECTOR

By selecting an individual slide you can access the Slide Inspector. This allows you to set up functionality on a slide-by-slide basis.

Using the General tab, you can alter the duration of an individual slide or choose to have it pause by the use of the Manual Advance setting. You can also choose an audio file for the individual slide. Keep in mind that by doing this the overall audio file will no longer function.

THE SLIDESHOW VIEWER

Above the Slideshow Editor is the Viewer which enables you to test out your slideshow. By using the four available buttons (Play/Pause, Stop, Skip Forward, and Skip Reverse), you can watch the presentation and make immediate adjustments.

Note that using the viewer eliminates any pauses you may have added. So in order to fully test out the presentation you will need to use the simulator.

SAVE

As always, make sure you save (Command-S) before continuing.

Now you have a basic understanding of how slideshows are made. The next section explains how all our authored assets are linked together to create a fully navigational DVD.

▸ STEP 5: LINKING ASSETS

We're in the home stretch now. At this point everything in our DVD Project has been imported and manipulated for our purposes. The final task that remains before it can be multiplexed is the linking of the assets.

In this section you will create all the relationships between the buttons and the menus, tracks, and slideshow.

We should first refresh our memories by consulting the flowchart we created earlier (*see page 36*). This will act as a guide for all the links. Starting from the top, we will work our way through the various channels. This should be a rather easy process given the fact that all our menus, tracks, and slideshows are prepared and ready to be connected.

The only fields we will be dealing with in the Property Inspectors are:

- ▸ Target in the individual Button Inspectors
- ▸ End Jump in the Track Inspectors
- ▸ End Jump in the Slideshow Inspector

MAIN MENU

We'll start with the Main Menu. Select it in the Outline Tab or choose it from the Viewer pull-down menu. You should see the menu with the three buttons we created earlier: Play Movie, Sc. Selection, Sp. Features.

Starting at the top, click on the Play Movie button to access the Button Inspector.

Use the Target pull-down menu and locate the Feature (Target > Tracks > Feature > Track).

You will be offered a list of all the Track Markers in order. The first marker (track) is the start of the track. In this case, you could also select Vacation (Target > Tracks > Main Feature > Vacation) which is also the start of the track.

Continue on to the next button down which is Scene Selection. Select it to access its Inspector. Once again, use the Target pull-down menu and locate the Sc. Selection menu and choose either (Menu) or Vacation from the list of buttons in the menu (Target > Menus > Sc. Selection Menu > Menu) or (Target > Menus > Sc. Selection Menu > Vacation).

To complete authoring the Main Menu, select the Special Features button and select its Target (Target > Menus > Sp. Features Menu > Menu) or (Target > Menus > Sp. Features Menu > Behind the Scenes).

Having completed these links you are finished with the Main Menu.

SCENE SELECTION MENU

Our next menu to author is the Scene Selection menu. This is accessed from the Main Menu and contains buttons that allow us to jump to specific scenes in the movie. There are six of these chapter buttons as well as a button to return us to the Main menu.

Start with the Vacation button. Select it to
access the Inspector and use the Target field to
locate and choose the Vacation marker in the
Feature Track listing (Target > Tracks > Feature >
Vacation).

Do the same for the Dumped button (Target
> Tracks > Feature > Dumped) and all the rest of
the chapter buttons.

For the Main Menu button you want to link back to the Main Menu.
Once you've located the Main Menu in the Target field you can choose to
return to the menu or to any specific button on the Main Menu. Because the
last button selected on the Main Menu was the Scene Selection button, I
thought it would be good to have the Special
Features button selected (that is, the next button
down on the list) when we return to the Main
Menu (Target > Menus > Main Menu > Sp.
Features).

*This is where you can really flex your muscles as a DVD designer. In ear-
lier versions of DVD Studio Pro you only had the option to return to the first
button in the menu. With the advances of version 2 you can now return to the
menu and choose which button is selected. The theory behind this is that it
maintains a certain flow as you navigate through the DVD.*

If you are watching all the special features in order it would be a drag to
have to scroll down the list every time you jumped back to the Main Menu
when the selection was finished. Pre-selecting the next option for the viewer
is a more intuitive navigational design and I highly recommend it. This is
not to say that you can't choose it for some menus and not for others.
Conventional wisdom says that after the Main Feature is over it jumps back
to the Main Menu with Play Movie selected.

SPECIAL FEATURES MENU

The Special Features menu has connections to various elements. Behind the
Scenes and Trailer are both tracks, the Director's Commentary links to
the feature with an alternate audio file, Cast & Crew Bios connects to
another sub-menu, and Stills Gallery accesses a slideshow. We will link these

in order. By now you should have a good understanding of the process. Remember the first thing you need to do before you can choose the Target is to select the appropriate button in the Menu Viewer.

Link the Behind the Scenes button with the Behind the Scenes track (Target > Tracks > Behind the Scenes > Track) and link the Trailer button with its corresponding track (Target > Tracks > Trailer > Track).

The next button is labeled Director's Commentary. I've decided that when you activate this option, the movie will automatically begin with the Director's Commentary instead of the original soundtrack. In order to author this you need to do two things. First of all, you must select its target, in this case the Main Feature (Target > Tracks > Feature > Track).

We've now instructed the DVD to access the movie, but it will still play the default audio in the A1 Stream: STRANDED-Feature.AC3. In order to force it to play the feature with the Commentary track it must be instructed to override it.

In the Advanced tab of the Button Inspector is a section entitled Streams which allows you to select an Angle, Audio, and/or Subtitle Stream that is utilized when this specific button is activated.

In our case we want the Commentary file (STRANDED-Comm.AC-3) that currently resides in the A2 Stream in the Features Track editor.

Simply use the Audio pull-down menu and select the desired Stream: Audio Stream 2. Now when you activate the Director's Commentary button the movie will play with the Commentary track.

According to the flowchart, the Cast & Crew button needs to link to the Cast & Crew Bios sub-menu. (Target > Menus > C&C Bios Menu > Writer/Director).

The Stills Gallery button accesses the slideshow that we created (Target > Slideshows > Still Gallery > Slideshow). As mentioned before, you could also choose the first slide in the group as well.

The last button in the group is the Main Menu button. This allows the viewer to return to the Main page after they have viewed everything or if there is nothing further that interests them. I've decided that when the viewer returns to the Main Menu the Play Movie button should be selected (Target > Menus > Main Menu > Menu).

CAST & CREW BIOS MENU

The Cast & Crew Bios menu needs to link to our Bios sub-menus. There are four different options plus the ability to return to the originating menu (Special Features) instead of returning to the Main Menu.

I will demonstrate one of these; simply repeat the process for the rest. The first button is Writer/Director. This accesses the Writer/Director sub-menu (Target > Menus > C&C Bios Menu > Writer/Director).

The Features button returns us to the Special Features menu. I've decided that it should have the next button (Stills Gallery Button) on the Menu selected when it returns (Target > Menus > Sp. Features Menu > Stills Gallery).

INDIVIDUAL CAST & CREW BIOS

Each one of these bios has two buttons: Next and Back. The Next button advances you to the following bio (instead of having to return to the Cast & Crew Bios menu to access it from there). The Back button, in the case of the Writer/Director menu, will return you to the Cast & Crew Bios menu. On the other menus it should return you to the previous bio.

These examples represent the buttons for the Writer/Director menu. The Next button should link to the Producer's Bio menu's Next button (Target > Menus > Producer Bio > Next) and the Back button should return us to the Cast & Crew Bios menu's Producer button (Target > Menus >C&C Bios Menu > Producer).

END JUMP

At this point all the menu buttons are linked and functioning, but we're not finished yet. We have three tracks (Main Feature, Behind the Scenes, and Trailer) plus a Slideshow: Stills Gallery that need instructions on what to do when they are finished playing. This is known as the End Jump setting and it works in the same way as the Target Field.

TRACKS

Let's look at the individual tracks first. Select the Feature in either the Outline Tab or in the Viewer. The End Jump field is located at the top of the Track Inspector.

FEATURE

When the movie is over it is customary to return to the Main Menu. So, as we did with the Button targets, select the Main Menu in the End Jump pull-down menu. (End Jump > Menus > Main Menu > Menu).

BEHIND THE SCENES

The Behind the Scenes Featurette is accessed from the Special Features menu, so it goes without saying that it should return there. We've already discussed making the intuitive decision to return to the next successive button, in this case the Trailer button (End Jump > Menus > Sp. Features Menu > Trailer).

TRAILER

Like the Behind the Scenes Featurette, the Trailer is linked to the Special Features menu as well. The next button on the list is for Director's Commentary, to which our End Jump should link (End Jump > Menus > Sp. Features Menu > Commentary).

At this point all the tracks are completely authored, leaving one last element to be linked: the Stills Gallery.

STILLS GALLERY

The End Jump field for the Stills Gallery is accessed from the Slideshow Inspector. Like the Behind the Scenes and Trailer tracks, when the Stills Gallery finishes it should return to the Special Features menu.

Because the Stills Gallery is the last button on the list (except for the Main Menu button), I've decided to have it return to the top of the options (Behind the Scenes button) instead of the Main Menu button. This is a personal preference, suggesting to viewers that they stick around in this menu instead of heading back to the main page so soon (End Jump > Menus > Sp. Features Menu > Behind The Scenes).

FINISHING TOUCHES

Believe it or not, but the *Stranded* DVD is now completely authored. When the process is broken down into easy-to-follow steps, it's not particularly difficult.

I suggest you save the project before continuing. The next section deals with testing the DVD project to make sure that everything is working as it should and then multiplexing, and ultimately burning, a watchable DVD.

▸ STEP 6: TESTING

Our project is completely authored, but before we rush off and drop some green to make tons of copies we should test it out first. This is of utmost importance. The last thing you need is a stack of a thousand DVDs that are only usable as coasters because you forgot to link the Play Feature button.

There are several different ways to check your project (some more involved than others) and each is important. There is the previewing of elements, the simulation, and the emulation of your project.

PREVIEWING

This method was touched upon in previous chapters. By using the Viewer Tab you have the ability to choose a track or slideshow to watch. This however only allows you to check for video and audio problems. You will not be able to test connectivity and button functions.

SIMULATION

DVD Studio Pro comes with a way to watch your DVD as you create it. The Simulator acts much like a DVD player (with many of the same controls and settings). It is accessible at any time during your construction and is a comprehensive way to test the navigation of your project.

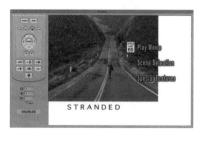

There are limitations, however. For instance, simulating a project in its early stages is fine, but if you haven't set any of the Target or End Jump settings, you're not going to get very far. Also, because the project has not yet been built, there is the potential for inappropriate pausing and stuttering which may lead you to believe there is a problem, when there really isn't.

Regardless, using the Simulator as much as possible during the construction is a wise choice. Even if you just want to see a simple menu operation it is worth the few seconds it takes. It also makes your life easier in the final testing. If you catch most of the mistakes early on, you won't be overwhelmed by a laundry list of small tweaks you may have to make at the end phase.

 To access the Simulator, either choose it from the toolbar or select it from the File pull-down menu (File > Simulate).

The Simulator Window will appear and the project will operate like a DVD you just put in a DVD player (assuming that your first play setting has been set). If you've done your work correctly, you should be able to navigate through all the menus and watch all the tracks and slideshows without any glitches or interruptions in your journey. Make sure you test every button and track to make sure the targets and end jumps are working properly.

It is of utmost importance that you test everything in your project. Even though you're probably sick and tired of seeing all the tracks at this point, it is crucial to check them thoroughly without making assumptions. You've invested a lot of time up to this point ; it's worht it to take another few hours to make sure that all your hard work was not in vain.

If your project runs smoothly, then you can feel confident that it is authored correctly and you should move on to the next phase of testing.

EMULATION

This testing process is the real deal, and also the most time consuming. The two emulation options are to either Build your project and watch it on your computer's DVD player or Build and Format your project and burn it onto a DVD-R so it can been viewed on a stand-alone DVD player as well.

This will absolutely let you know if your DVD project has been successfully authored and is an essential step before your have any copies made.

BUILDING YOUR PROJECT

The first part of transforming your project into a watchable DVD is known as the Build. This creates two folders (VIDEO_TS and AUDIO_TS) that contain all the DVD compliant files. During the Build all the menus are transformed into a single file and the tracks are multiplexed (or "muxed") from the separate video, audio and/or subtitle streams into a single Video Object file.

 In the Toolbar you have three options: Build, Format, and Build/Format.

BUILD

If you only plan to test on your computer's DVD player, select Build. You will be prompted to choose a place to store the VIDEO_TS and AUDIO_TS Folders. Remember when we first set up our project folders in the last chapter? I had you create a folder called AUDIO & VIDEO TS Files. This is the folder you want to select as their destination.

BUILD/FORMAT

If you are going to eventually burn a check disc, then choose Build/Format. A dialogue box will appear allowing you to select the Build destination as well as other format settings.

In the middle of the General tab is the Location field. Select the Choose button to find the AUDIO & VIDEO TS files folder.

At the bottom is where you can choose which output device you want to use to create the final burn. You may have multiple DVD burners or a DLT machine. Because we are interested in making our own DVD-R check disc to watch on a DVD player, we should choose a DVD burner as our device.

Use the DVD-R Simulation Mode only if you think there might be Buffer Underrun issues. It will proceed with the burning process without actually writing on the DVD-R.

The Lossless Linking box should be enabled if you believe you may need Buffer Underrun protection. Otherwise it should be left unchecked, especially if your are burning a DVD-R master for a replication facility.

Buffer Underrun — When data is sent to the DVD-R drive from the source disc, it must flow at a consistent rate to the drive's buffer in order to achieve a successful burn. But there can be an interruption of data due to the device's speed or an overloaded system trying to multitask too many requests at once. This will cause a buffer underrun error which will result in an unusable disc.

The Disc/Volumes and Region Copyright tabs contain settings that you've dealt with before. They are provided again in case you have not set them previously. The only major difference is the Volume Creation Date  which records the date and time the DVD was formatted.

PROGRESS BAR & LOG TAB

DVD Studio Pro will display a progress bar to show you where it is in the building process and a  Log to keep you updated on the build. Any Red or Yellow warnings will signal a problem in the build. If all goes well it will let you know at the conclusion of the build with the message Compile Completed Successfully.

When the build is complete you can check out your AUDIO & VIDEO TS files folder. There will be the two new folders: AUDIO_TS and VIDEO_TS.

The AUDIO_TS folder will be completely empty. You might think that it would contain your audio files but in fact it was designed for DVD-Audio. However, it is still necessary in order to to make your DVD function properly. Without that empty file your DVD will not work.

The VIDEO_TS folder contains all the DVD files, which are divided into three types: Video Manager files, Track Content files, and Layout files.

VIDEO MANAGER FILES

The Video Manager files contain navigational information and are broken down into three types:

- ▸ VIDEO_TS.IFO
- ▸ VIDEO_TS.BUP
- ▸ VIDEO_TS.VOB

The .IFO files contain most of the important information such as structure and capacity. The .BUP are in fact backup versions of the .IFO files in case any are corrupted and can't be read. They are also written in a different location to minimalize the chance of both files being unreadable. The .VOB files contain the actual media.

TRACK CONTENT FILES

There are at least four files created for each track, story or slideshow: one .IFO, one .BUP, and two .VOB files. One file will be created for the menus and at least one more for the content (because the maximum size of a .VOB file is 1GB in most cases there will be more than one .VOB content file, but no more than eight).

The first set begins with:

VTS_01_0.BUP
VTS_01_0.IFO
VTS_01_0.VOB
VTS_01_1.VOB

The second set would be:

VTS_02_0.BUP
VTS_02_0.IFO
VTS_02_0.VOB
VTS_02_1.VOB

LAYOUT FILES

There are two other files created during the Build: .layout file and a VOB_DATA.LAY file. These are non-standard files used by DVD Studio Pro and could cause problems if you choose to format and burn in another program.

BUILDING AND FORMATTING A DUAL-LAYERED PROJECT

If your project is dual-layered there are two extra settings that need to be addressed. One is the direction the second layer will be read by the DVD player and the other is where the break between the two layers will fall.

DUAL-LAYER DIRECTION

You have the option of choosing which direction the laser will read the second layer. The reason why this matters is that there is a slight pause when the laser switches layers. Which type you choose will determine how long that pause may be.

The first layer is always read from the inside (near the center hole) of the disc out (the outer edge). Your two options are PTP (Parallel Track Path) which reads the second layer exactly like the first (from the inside out), or OTP (Opposite Track Path) which reads from the outside edge in.

Naturally, if you choose the OTP method, the pause will be shorter. This is because once it reaches the end it can just start making its way back while reading off your disc, instead of having to physically travel back to the center to begin reading outwards again.

DUAL-LAYER BREAK POINT

Because a dual-layered disc does in fact have two layers, there has to be a place where Layer One ends and Layer Two begins. This is known as the Disc Break. If you are planning on using a DVD-9, then your project must have a disc break. Fortunately, within reason, you can decide where that is going to be.

But there are some rules that must be followed. First, the disc break has to fall on a Track Marker. If there are no markers where you want the layers to break, then you might have to place one there specifically for that purpose. Keep in mind that, depending on how much of the 7.95 GB you are using, the first layer will need to be filled up as much as possible first. So if you do place a marker it should be somewhere in the vicinity of 3.9 GB in (and no more).

For the least noticeable results it's best to place the break either between scene transitions or at a point where there is no dialogue. DVD Studio Pro will give you a list of suitable markers from which to choose.

If you find that you are having trouble locating a good place to break the layers, build the disc and look at the files in the VIDEO_TS folder. Items are written in the order of the Outline Tab. If push comes to shove, you can rearrange the order of the Outline Tab to force a certain track or marker to fall within the Disc Break usable zone.

DVD Studio Pro also has the ability to decide where the Disc Break will be for you. It basically accesses how much space you're actually using and targets an area in the 3.9 GB zone of the first layer. It then looks for the closest marker. If there isn't one, DVD Studio Pro will alert you that there is no marker available, but it will also tell you where one should be placed in order to complete the formatting.

BURNING THE TEST DISC

When you choose to build and format to a DVD-R you will immediately be prompted to insert a useable DVD-R into the disc drive.

It is highly recommended to cough up the dough and use a quality brand disc. Even though they are inexpensive and you are using this only as a test, unbranded media can be unreliable and give you a false sense that there are problems that don't exist. You've invested the time so invest the money as well and use a DVD-R that is going to give you the proper results.

Once you have the test disc, treat it with care. These discs are unfortunately very fragile and prone to scratches as well as fingerprints. Test the disc out on a stand-alone DVD player first. If for some reason the disc is not recognized, don't panic. The player may not have the ability to play your DVD-R. Older models are especially prone to this. Before doing anything else, I recommend trying it out on a newer DVD player.

We're going to assume that you've done a masterful job creating your DVD project and your Main Menu is currently staring back at you. This is where the real test begins.

I suggest you throw on some comfortable clothes, grab something to snack on and dim the lights (don't turn them off because you're going to need to take notes if everything doesn't go as planned).

It's good to create a check list of things to look out for. I suggest having a list of all your menus and their buttons as well as a listing of all the tracks.

TESTING MENUS

These are the things you should be looking for in regards to the menus:

- ▸ Overall look of the menu (title-safe areas)
- ▸ Overall look of the buttons in all their states
- ▸ Intuitive button flow (when you navigate with the remote control arrows the item you mentally expect to be next is selected)
- ▸ Button functionality (the buttons go where they are supposed to when activated)
- ▸ Can you access every menu, track, and slideshow with the Buttons

TESTING TRACKS

These are the things you should be looking for in regards to the tracks:

- ▸ Overall picture quality
- ▸ Overall sound quality
- ▸ End Jumps are functional
- ▸ Chapters are in the right place (if applicable)
- ▸ Remote buttons work (i.e. menu, skip track, audio, subtitle, etc.)

TESTING SLIDESHOWS

These are the things you should be looking for in regards to the slideshows:

- ▸ Overall picture quality
- ▸ Overall sound quality (if applicable)
- ▸ Automatic progression of slides work as well as manual progression
- ▸ End Jumps are functional

If you find there are things that are authored correctly but feel counter-intuitive when you watch them, I suggest changing them and re-building the DVD project. You shouldn't settle for good enough due to laziness. It's exciting to get it done, but it's worth the extra time to get it right. Remember your reputation is on the line when you release a project like this. Your friends and family might be forgiving of a small glitch, but the guy who shells out the twenty bucks or more for your title certainly won't appreciate a half-ass job.

TESTING A DUAL-LAYERED DVD

One of the major drawbacks to making a dual-layered DVD is that currently you cannot burn a dual-layered DVD-R. Other than being a major drag, the other big problem is how to test the disc before you send it off to be replicated.

Fortunately there are some options. First off really put your nose to the grindstone when you simulate the project in DVD Studio Pro. It can have its pitfalls but you will certainly know if your navigation and buttons are working correctly, which is a big part of testing. You'll get a good sense of the video and if you have a good sound system hooked up to your computer (most computer surround systems are very affordable these days), you'll be able to check out your sound as well.

Another, more radical option is to make low bit-rate versions of all your video files so that they will fit on a single-layered DVD-5. The drawbacks are obvious. You'll have no clue of how your actual video will look nor how the layer change will function. This is also a time-consuming project too because you have to re-encode all your video, which will also take up valuable hard drive space as well. One way to have your cake and eat it too with the low bit-rate disc is to create two high bit-rate discs that only contain the video and audio. Once again, though, you will have to author these separately and it will take a large chunk of time.

You can also build your project to your computer's hard drive as a Disc Image. This will allow you to play it with the computer's DVD player. There are two drawbacks: You will only be able to view it on your computer, and there is no way for the computer to emulate the disc break, so you will not be able to to see how that will look.

Unfortunately, your best option is to trust in yourself. If you did your homework correctly than you should have nothing to worry about. You can easily retrace your steps through the DVD project and make sure that everything was done properly.

When it comes time to replicate the DVD (you can only reproduce DVD-9's through replication), insist on a Check Disc struck from the Glass Master. If there is a problem, you may have to pay extra to have a new Glass Master made after you've fixed the problem (possibly $200 or more), but that's certainly better than spending thousands of dollars on boxes of unusable DVDs.

NEARING THE FINISH LINE

At this point you should have successfully built your DVD and tested it completely for errors. You now have to decide how your are going to share your DVD with the world.

▸ STEP 7: MANUFACTURING

Once you have a finished project that has been thoroughly tested, it's time to deal with how you're planning to make copies. You basically have three options: make them yourself, have duplicates made, or have them replicated. All three options have pros and cons.

HOMEMADE DVD

If you only need a small number of DVDs, then it might be most cost effective to make them yourself by individually burning them through your computer. If you choose this route you are going to want to use high-quality media and a reliable DVD burner. You will also need to figure out how you want to package them.

Given that home-burned DVD-Rs have a tendency to be fickle in certain DVD players, anything you can do to maximize the quality of your finished DVD is in your best interest. It's highly recommended that you verify each disc to make sure that there are no technical flaws and at least check to make sure that they play before sending them out.

Another thing you will need to consider is the time factor. Burning a single disc can take an hour or more, especially if you are verifying it as well. Add the time it takes to check each disc and package it and you're talking a chunk of time and that's just for one DVD.

Speaking of packaging, you should consider how the final product will look if you just plan to print out case wraps on your computer. More importantly, because you shouldn't put adhesive labels on DVDs (they can screw up the balance and cause playback problems), you'll have to figure out how to label your discs. If you want them in Amaray cases and shrink-wrapped, there's another cost consideration too.

There are desktop machines you can buy that will actually make copies and print labels on them as well but they are expensive. Unless you plan on doing this consistently it's probably not worth the investment.

Pros
- ▸ Keep costs down if you need a small amount
- ▸ Can be manufactured on demand

Cons
- ▸ Unreliability of DVD-R Media
- ▸ Price per manufactured DVD is high (disc media and packaging)
- ▸ Time-consuming process
- ▸ Wear and tear on your DVD burner
- ▸ Quality of packaging
- ▸ Does not support Copy Protection or Region Coding
- ▸ Can only duplicate single-layer DVDs

DUPLICATION

This is the same concept as the homemade DVDs except on a bigger scale. There are companies that are set up to make multiple copies of DVDs as well as label and package them. The advantage to having a company duplicate your disc is that you are not locked into any minimums. Just know that the fewer you get, the more you will pay per unit.

Even though you've eliminated many of the cons of doing it at home (such as printing and packaging), these are still duplicated DVDs and are subject to the same unreliability as the ones you burn yourself.

When choosing a duplication facility, make sure that they use good quality disc media and that they stand by their finished product. I highly suggest you use a place that provides you with a check disc that not only shows the quality of the media but also the quality of the printing on the disc surface. Most places provide up to five-color printing. (The fifth color is a white background that covers up the silver disc surface.)

Keep in mind too that, depending on how busy they are, you may have to wait a number of weeks to get your product.

Pros
- You can choose the quantity
- Someone else is doing the work
- High-quality packaging

Cons
- Unreliability of DVD-R Media
- Price per manufactured DVD is potentially high (depending on how many units)
- It may take weeks to get your product
- Duplication does not support Copy Protection or Region Coding
- Can only duplicate single-layer DVDs

REPLICATION

This is the professional process of making DVD copies and the one used by the studios. The advantages are many but so are the disadvantages. How this differs from duplication is in how the DVDs are copied. Instead of just reproducing the material onto another pre-made disc, a Glass Master is made that literally stamps newly formed DVDs out of molten plastic. The Glass Master can then be stored away and new copies made with it at any time.

Because of the way they are manufactured, a replicated DVD will play on all DVD players and support copy protection and region encoding. Replication also supports your ability to make dual-layered DVDs.

As great as all that sounds there are some things to consider. First off, though many replication facilities now accept DVD-Rs as a master copy, they are notoriously unreliable for making a Glass Master. Most companies will suggest you give them your project on a DLT which is fine and dandy if you happen to have a DLT machine. If you don't, it can be expensive to have someone make one for you. Also, you really want to make sure that your project is completely tested, because if there is an authoring problem found after the Glass Master is made (the check disc is struck from the Glass Master), you will have to pay to have a new Glass Master made, in essence starting from scratch again.

DLT (Digital Linear Tape) — This tape format is the standard of the DVD industry and is by far the most reliable format used to master a DVD. It also supports the ability to make dual-layered DVDs by having each layer on a separate tape. The problem is that DLT machines can be pricey and so is the media (a single DLT can cost about $50). There are companies that will transfer your project to a DLT but that can be pricey too.

If you plan to make a living off of authoring DVDs, it's worth investing in a DLT machine. Brand new they can run you in the thousands, but older models like the Quantum DLT 2000 or 4000 can be purchased used for a few hundred dollars which could potentially be cheaper than paying someone for a one-time transfer.

A typical minimum order for replicated DVDs is 1,000 units, but they only run you about $1.25 per unit completely printed, packaged, and shrink wrapped! I know that sounds great but there are some extra costs.

The Glass Master will run you about $200. Having any paper inserts inside the disc will cost you for printing and insertion. Also, there is a little thing called overage. Because of the way the replication machines work, it is hard to make exactly 1,000 DVDs, so there are typically extra discs that are manufactured (around 10% more is average). Well, guess what folks, you are responsible to pay for those extra discs whether you want them or not. Make sure that you add an extra 10% into your budget just for this. You may get lucky and have only about ten or more, but I've had runs that had an extra 130 DVDs and that's a chunk of change.

Replication can also be a time-consuming process. Many of the smaller facilities are not set up for multiple projects so they stagger them using certain times for creating glass masters and striking check discs. Because of this a process that typically takes ten to 15 business days may take up to a month or more. You must remember that when they get you the check disc, it's up to you to review it and authorize them to continue with the replication process. If you drag your ass, it slows up the process.

Pros

▸ Top-quality manufacturing and packaging
▸ Relatively low cost per unit
▸ Supports dual-layered DVDs
▸ Supports copy protection and region coding

Cons

▸ Minimum of 1,000 units
▸ High set-up fees
▸ Potential of paying for overages
▸ Takes time for replication (up to a month or more)
▸ May have to provide DLT for mastering

DVD is authored and replicated. Now it's time to activate your marketing campaign.

Section 5

CREATIVE MARKETING DRIVES DVD SALES

Now that you've made your feature, carefully planned the DVD release, followed the steps in the previous sections to author it, and had it replicated, how will it reach an audience? In other words, how do you get potential customers to buy the DVD and watch it on their DVD player or computer?

In another word, marketing. Marketing will be your most important tool to get exposure for your film and increase sales. Case in point: Mediocre Hollywood movies sell millions of copies at retail on a regular basis. The studios have a marketing machine in place that allows them access to major retailers and a budget that can create awareness on a massive scale through aggressive online, print, and television campaigns.

Your challenge will be to match the quality of a major DVD release with your packaging and advertising, while using simple grassroots and guerilla marketing techniques to get the word out to your potential audience. Every film is unique, which will affect your creative approach along with your target audience. All projects, however, require the same basic ingredients in order to succeed.

A separate book would be needed to cover the subject of sales and marketing in depth. A title that I strongly recommend is Mark Steven Bosko's *The Complete Independent Movie Marketing Handbook*. Bosko's book is the ultimate guide to the finer details of film marketing. Use it as a companion title to this book, as it expands on areas that we have limited space to explore in the following section.

INGREDIENTS OF A SUCCESSFUL MARKETING CAMPAIGN

All marketing campaigns for a DVD release will include the following components:

Packaging — The DVD sleeve itself is a marketing piece, since it is what the consumer will see displayed in stores. It's also useful to know that packaging often determines which titles buyers decide to carry in their stores. People *do* judge a book by its cover.

Publicity, Press, and Promotion — There are two types of publicity, one for the trades (the industry) and one intended for consumers. Press releases timed to hit consumer and trade press at key moments, along with promotions such as contests, are the most cost-effective way to reach buyers and less expensive than advertising. Remember, an inch of press is worth a full page of advertising. These three "Ps" work hand in hand to create aware-ness and demand for your DVD.

Reviews — Quotes from prominent critics and media outlets are a key element in boosting your film's marketability.

Advertising — Again, two campaigns apply here as well, consumer and trade. For the most part, advertising in mainstream print publications is prohibitively expensive. Online advertising, on the other hand, can reach far more potential purchasers for less money and the campaign can be better targeted.

Timing — Timing is really an x-factor component that can help an independent DVD title succeed in the marketplace by planning a release date around a synergistic event or a similar mainstream title.

We'll explore each of these elements in greater depth in the following section.

DVD PACKAGING — THE POWER OF THE SLEEVE

The DVD sleeve should be the best possible representation of your movie. One philosophy states: "*Make a work of art, but sell it like porn.*"

No matter how unique you think your movie is, the marketplace is filled with other titles, many just like yours. Independent films share shelf space with very aggressive packaging from studio marketing. You have to compete with the studios and make your DVD sleeve stand out. How do you make your packaging have an impact when you most likely only have a few seconds of a potential buyer's attention?

One element in your favor is your title's uniqueness and freshness to the DVD audience. Even an independent film more than five years old is new to someone who has never heard of it. Audiences hungry for new releases are often curious about new titles. Independent films are also a hot commodity. Twenty years ago, that was not the case. In a world seemingly dominated by studio action films and comedies, independent films have now become part of a regular moviegoer's diet. There are sections of video stores dedicated solely to independent movies, so now it's time to turn your weakness into a strength by capitalizing on what you have.

Begin by marketing your film as if it were new. That starts with quotes from critics and other credible people who will endorse the quality of your film. A quote on the front cover of the film from a champion — which doesn't have to be a movie critic — will grab people's attention.

FIND A CHAMPION

The single most important thing a filmmaker can do to get attention for their DVD is to find a champion. A champion can be a film critic or reviewer, a well-known filmmaker, or someone who speaks with some level of credibility when it comes to the content of the film. A champion provides a quote or endorsement touting the virtues of the movie, and this can be used to help secure a sale. For indie films with no stars, finding the "right" champion just may be the difference between getting a distribution deal or ending up as one of the thousands of cine-orphans without distribution in place.

One young Michigan filmmaker brought his low-budget horror film to the Cannes film market in the early 1980s. After failing to attract attention for his gruesome movie, he happened to run into horror novelist Stephen King. The wide-eyed young filmmaker begged King to attend a screening of his little independent movie. King agreed and liked it so much that he provided a quote which was used on the poster. The quote read:

> "*The most ferociously original horror movie of the year.*"
> — Stephen King, author of *Carrie* and *The Shining*

That quote from a best-selling author was used on all the film's marketing and posters. Just those few words from King put this little indie movie on the map. Michigan filmmaker Sam Raimi credits the quote that King provided for *Evil Dead* for helping launch his career. The secret is to come up with a champion that breaks convention and gets audiences (or distributors) interested in seeing the film. Securing a "thumbs up" from Roger Ebert is, let's be honest, a long shot at best. Being creative about exactly who to approach is critical.

But the champion doesn't need to be a critic. The feature-length documentary *Starwoids* already had a great sales angle: you know, *Star Wars*. More than a few people have heard of that film. But how do you sell a documentary? Asking DVD consumers to watch an entertaining doc can be like asking a kid to eat vegetables. We had to get creative. We knew we needed someone to endorse the film and give it even more credibility. Someone who could elevate an already great doc and make it a must-see. We approached notorious indie filmmaker Kevin Smith. To fans, he perfectly represents the *Star Wars* generation. Smith liked the film enough to record some voice-over narration and even provided a ten-minute interview about the influence of *Star Wars* on his own films, which became an extra on the DVD. With Kevin Smith's endorsement, selling *Starwoids* became a lot easier. His affiliation gave the film the credibility to get into major retail chains like Best Buy.

WRITING COPY THAT SELLS

I cringe when I read poorly written descriptions of movies on the backs of DVDs. Often the descriptions of these independent films are either amateurishly written or so pretentious or vague, it's impossible to even tell what the movie is about. These short descriptive paragraphs are an essential piece of movie marketing and are one of the few things a DVD buyer has to rely on to decide whether to purchase your film. Here are a few writing tips that will help you to write eye-catching copy.

First and foremost, the description is not a review. Let's face it, it's advertising. Your movie description should include hyperbole that is honest — the average consumer has to care about a story that's engaging. You'll need to hone your writing skills by using your thesaurus. A lot. And if you're like most broke filmmakers and don't own a thesaurus, you can get a free one on the web at *www.dictionary.com.* (Or visit the public library.)

Begin by sprinkling your description with "emotional" language like *compelling, touching, moving, milestone, life-affirming, sexy, romantic, groundbreaking, heartfelt,* hey, use your own thesaurus! Adjectives like these do work, so use them liberally. Yes, it's hype and it can be very successful. A compelling description of the story should run between 100 and 200 words. The most important thing to remember is to be specific — tell the story, but never give away the ending. The story description should act as a tease without giving away too much. It's actually more difficult to write something short than something long, so make every word count.

OTHER COMPONENTS OF THE DVD SLEEVE

Award Mentions — Your DVD sleeve should also include a mention of any awards the film may have won. But be careful: if the festival or award is from a somewhat obscure source, you may be doing yourself more damage than good by including a mention on the cover. These kinds of awards are best noted by a graphic on the back of the sleeve.

Quotes — The back of the sleeve might contain more quotes and a few more images from the movie — but don't make the photos too small.

Special Features List — Include a box that stands out from the rest of the design that lists the special features that are on the DVD.

Technical Specifications — In that same box, include a "tech specs" that details single or double layer, running time, sound 5.1, other languages, etc. This is generally for DVD geeks, who will also be a large percentage of your audience, so give them what they want. And don't forget your website as well as your copyright info.

Ultimately you need to punch people in the face with your graphics. Your primary image should be so striking that it will compel someone to pick it up and look at it. Use bold and striking colors but avoid black, which tends to blend into the background on retail shelves. Black can sometimes work, but before you finalize your cover, test it. And whatever you do, avoid clichés like seeing your main characters' surprised faces as they look through a woman's sexy legs.

Ten Elements of Great DVD Sleeve Design

According to professional movie poster designer Jon C. Allen, follow these simple rules and you are on your way to memorable packaging.

1. Invoke feelings. Create some sort of emotion. This can be done through color, image, etc. A great design sparks interest, makes people stop. For example, a poster for a comedy should make you laugh.

2. Well thought-out typography. Type should complement the image, yet not attract undue attention to itself, and it should work with the imagery as a unit.

3. Second read. In other words, something you don't notice the first time you look at it. For example, take a look at the FedEx logo. Have you ever noticed the hidden arrow inside the type?

4. Good photography. Head strips of actors' heads on doubles' bodies sometimes work, but it's always nice to have an idea for a photo shoot, have that actors shot the way you envisioned, and use the resulting photography to make your design work.

5. Great tagline. Always important, especially for comedies. "Four Score and Seven Beers Ago..." made my *Senior Trip* poster work.

6. Title logo. A logo should stand on its own. A great logo complements the design and works well in its own context, because it will often be used on its own in other media, such as trailers. The logo should actually complement the poster, instead of "floating" out in front of the poster, as if it weren't part of the artwork.

7. Translatable. The design should translate well to other formats. Some things may look great at 27" x 41" on a movie poster, but how will it look on your DVD sleeve or on websites, or in black and white in a newspaper? Also, keep in mind that people who buy your DVD online will see your cover as the size of a postage stamp. The sleeve should also be striking when seen small.

8. Relevant to the film's story/plot. Sometimes a DVD cover has nothing to do with anything that happens in a film — for example, an idea may service the marketing, while being completely removed from the film itself.

9. Show something new. This is always a tricky issue. Movie posters mirror the movies themselves — it's rare that something new is tried as opposed to giving them what they've seen before.

10. Hit the target. It should please the intended audience. Know your demographic and be sure the poster appeals to this group. Studios not only hold focus groups for movies, but for the DVD cover as well.

10 Most Common Mistakes of Poster Design
These mistakes result in amateurish DVD covers and poor design.

1. "Kitchen sink" design.
2. Not thinking conceptually.
3. "It looks cool" being a design's only redeeming quality.
4. Thinking of it as art, instead of *commercial* art — it's about marketing, not just what looks good.
5. Not positioning the film well.

6. Not designing everything to work together. For example, typography not working with the imagery.

7. Unwillingness to compromise for the best overall design. Sure, there are compromises left and right, some of which will drive the designer crazy. Every designer has had the client change their "vision" and felt it was a fatal mistake. But that's the nature of the business; you're trying to market a movie. Being able to play within those boundaries and produce something worthwhile is part of the challenge.

8. Not using all the available elements to produce good work: typography, layout, color, imagery, concept.

9. Bad finishing skills. Sure, you have a brilliant idea that will make you the next Saul Bass (look up his posters for a treat), but the fact that it looks like crap because you aren't comfortable in Adobe PhotoShop will hinder your idea.

10. Not pleasing the client. Sure, it's easy to dismiss them if you don't agree with their opinions, but since they are paying you to market their movie, you should work with them, not against them.

CHEAP MARKET RESEARCH FOR YOUR DVD SLEEVE

When you're closely involved with a project, sometimes it's hard to see things that are obvious to others, so it's important to get feedback. Studios spend hundreds of thousands of dollars on focus groups for packaging, posters, and marketing campaigns. You can get the same benefit of their research and save hundreds of thousands of dollars if you are willing to spend some time loitering! Print out several different versions of your DVD sleeve and slip the artwork into a standard DVD amaray case. Walk into a Tower, Best Buy, Blockbuster, or your local mom-and-pop video store and nonchalantly place your DVD on the appropriate shelf. Now just stand back and watch. If you are really bold, put it strategically on the bottom shelf to see if anyone notices.

I recommend going on a Tuesday because this is when new DVD releases come out. In fact, the biggest film fanatics go on Tuesdays, and usually at lunch time, to pick up the new releases. Visit several places, wait, and watch what people say. See if they pick it up and read the back or even try to buy your movie. Then ask them for a moment of their time to ask them what drew them to your DVD. Try showing them several different versions of your cover if you are conflicted about which to use. This incredibly valuable input will either boost your confidence or send you back to the drawing board.

It's important to size up exactly who is offering their opinion. An 80-year-old woman who despises the cover for your "violent" movie is not someone you want to take seriously. Get comments from those people who fit your intended audience. If it really helps, have them fill out a quick questionnaire and even enter them in a drawing to get a free DVD, any gimmick to get their thoughts, as long as it doesn't take up more than a few minutes. (Be careful not to annoy customers too much; you don't want to get thrown out of the store. It does help to make friends with the DVD buyer for that store and even consider asking for their thoughts.) If you repeatedly get feedback that requires dramatic changes, be willing to rethink your concept and marketing materials entirely. The few days you spend doing this will prove invaluable. And be sure to take any feedback from consumers with a grain of salt; it's just a collection of opinions.

See the Resources section in the back of the book for a DVD sleeve example.

POWERFUL PUBLICITY, PRESS, AND PROMOTION

The press release is important because it's your opportunity to write about your film in the way you would like others to write about it. As someone who reads press releases daily, I can tell you that it is really important to write a press release that stands out.

The press release is your best tool in dealing with the media. In a sense, you're holding the hand of the journalists reading the release and helping them come up with a way to write about your DVD. Media people are barraged with press releases, hundreds weekly, so what is it about your press release that is going to make an impression? And what angle are you going to use to get them excited about your title? Your first press release should be an "announcement" of your title coming to DVD, proclaiming that you have either signed a deal with a distributor or that you are self-distributing your movie on DVD. In the press release, include a snappy headline and some sort of angle that makes the story worthwhile for media outlets to write about. Unique quotes will definitely get you attention as editors will use those quotes in their stories about your film.

I can't emphasize enough how important the writing is for your release. I'll tell you from experience that people in the media are lazy, because they're hit with this stuff on a constant basis, so prepare yourself for a shocking truth — most of the entertainment "news" that you read is actually cleverly regurgitated press releases. That's what most entertainment "news" is. Publicists who excel at press release writing are, in effect, running the entertainment news media. So if you're really good at writing a press release, you have the opportunity to write your own press. It's shocking how many journalists (so-called "entertainment journalists") and reviewers will regurgitate and re-use the same adjectives and synopses they read in a press kit in their own writing. You have the opportunity to take advantage of this by writing smart press releases.

Your next press release will announce that the DVD is, in fact, released. You might want to include something for certain media members, like pointing out where the DVD Easter eggs that are hidden. It's yet another angle for them to write about your film. You'll want to include a "Press Only" area of your website where press releases and images from your DVD will be included for media types to crib. And believe me, they will use that material, so spend the time to make it great.

See the Resources section in the back of the book for a DVD press release template.

REVIEWS — GETTING KILLER QUOTES

Your plan should include well-timed DVD screener copies sent to members of the press who are receptive to your film's particular genre. Always look for an angle that will make your title stand out. But be warned: reviewers are sought after constantly for coverage from filmmakers and publicists. Hounding them by email or phone will only create ill will that could affect the review. Hiring a publicist who is well versed in dealing with the press is money well spent. Media types can be touchy at times since they are barraged by requests to cover product, so a delicate approach will produce better results. However, if those funds are unavailable, directly approaching a receptive writer from a particular print or online publication is recommended.

To drum up your own press, post on message boards where people talk about film or talk about independent DVD. Your posts will create awareness;

again, just don't annoy. You can even post a review of your own film where it is listed online at places like Amazon.com. Of course, it does helps if the review is legitimate; but you may also re-post a review from another outlet there.

MAXIMIZE ADVERTISING

Advertising comes in the form of a two-pronged marketing campaign — one is marketing you pay for and the other is marketing you don't pay for. If you have disposable funds, several thousand at least, it is in your best interests to advertise where you feel your target market will best discover your film.

There are countless great websites that would be a perfect place to advertise your film. Use *Alexa.com*, a website that acts as kind of a Nielsen ratings for the internet, to help you choose where best to advertise online. For dollars spent in relation to eyeballs reached, there is no better place to advertise than online. Look especially for websites that feature reviews of independent films. And there are more inexpensive places to advertise online than you would expect, *Film Threat* being one of them. Create a series of banner ads to use online in the sizes 720x90, 468x60, 120x60, 120x120, and so on. These ads can also be used to trade with other websites. (More on that later.)

Consider that if you advertise, it is not out of line to ask that the film be reviewed during your ad run. It is the sure way to guarantee a media outlet will review your film. Now, it's important to be respectful of the walls between editorial and advertising; you can only expect that the film will be reviewed fairly. In the end, buying advertising will not buy a positive review. In fact, the less pressure you apply, the better the outcome is likely to be.

If you cannot afford $5,000 or $25,000 or any amount for advertising, then you'll have to get creative. Marketing that you don't pay for is better known as guerilla or grassroots marketing. When you need to advertise, and dollars are not at your disposal, you have three options:

1. Trade-out advertising
2. Barter advertising
3. Per inquiry advertising

Trade-out involves offering free ads on your website for ads on another website. This is the most difficult type to negotiate, but if you have film-making friends, this kind of exposure can't hurt.

Barter advertising involves offering something in return for advertising, which could be DVDs or some other service or material item you can offer the outlet where you wish to advertise.

Per inquiry advertising is less common. It involves paying the advertising only on a "per inquiry" basis. So, for each DVD that you sell, you pay the media outlet money for that sale.

For the most part, media outlets prefer cash advertisers only. But during slow periods of the year, there always exists a certain amount of unsold space and a media outlet can either give that space to a public service announcement or they could negotiate terms with you.

GOOD TIMING

Timing is always an x-factor that, when used to your advantage, can increase sales dramatically. Timing is also the easiest marketing tool to take advantage of. If you have a film with a seasonal theme — Christmas, Easter, Halloween — it stands to reason that the best time to hit the shelves would be just before those holidays.

Additionally, if you have an actor in your film who also happens to be the star of a blockbuster film hitting DVD, time your release on the heels of the mainstream release. Interest in that particular actor will be high and this is the moment to take advantage of that. For example, when *Starwoids* was released to DVD, we made sure that the on-sale date was one week before *Star Wars Episode I* hit store shelves. This fortuitous timing led to Best Buy putting in a large order for the film. Look for any possible timing advantages when you choose your release date.

PRICE IS MARKETING

The price of your DVD is itself a form of marketing. Generally your MSRP (manufacturer's suggested retail price) is going to be $19.99. However, market research suggests that once a DVD title reaches a price point of $14.99 or lower, sales jump dramatically, because it becomes an impulse buy — it's less than twenty bucks. At this point, it becomes an issue of volume — would you like to sell more DVDs at a lower price or fewer DVDs at a higher price? Setting the price for your title is worth careful consideration.

UNCONVENTIONAL MARKETING METHODS

Less is more in the world of marketing independent films and not exactly by choice. With a tiny fraction of studio marketing budgets, indie distributors are expected to deliver as aggressive a campaign as the typical summer blockbuster. The challenge is to deliver a *creative* campaign at a fraction of the cost. The idea of actually competing head to head against a major DVD release is ludicrous. You must identify the niche for your title, then reach that group through grassroots marketing. Here are some specific examples, which should merely be a springboard for your own ideas.

Promote your DVD with a film festival screening

Consider partnering with a regional film festival which will support the DVD release with a special screening.

Have a DVD release party

Then line up a liquor sponsor and make everyone at your DVD release party happy.

Word-of-mouth screenings

Get your actors or the key crew to speak at a local college screening, which can also result in free press. The college film class gets the benefit of a free screening and you get the word of mouth.

Get a booth

Depending on your film, consider getting booth space at the Gay Pride Parade or at the San Diego Comic Con. Whatever audience you are targeting, there is an event where you can either pass out coupons or flyers or have a booth that promotes the film.

Free Stuff

Give away free T-shirts or hats to video stores who order more than a certain number of copies.

Contests

Have a contest giveaway. Even better, try to have the contest fit in with the theme of your film. If the film is a horror movie, give away a bucket of blood to 100 lucky winners. Okay, that's a little extreme, but you get the idea. The point is to be creative.

SAMPLE DVD SALES & MARKETING PLAN

Your marketing plan should kick off simultaneously with the production of the DVD. Don't wait until the DVD itself is ready for replication before you think about your strategy. Below is a sample plan for the DVD *Starwoids*. The title sold over 15,000 units at retail and continues to sell online. Here is a brief overview of the actual plan that was used to sell this film.

DVD Marketing Push
1. Contact distributor's key account list directly with new movie information
2. Develop a sales sheet for new DVD release with summary on back
3. Establish an ongoing relationship with major chains including online rental
4. Strengthen relationship with National Distributor
5. Establish relationship with additional smaller distributors
6. Get list of stores that bought similar titles and contact
7. Establish "warm" list (database) of video retailers that do not go through National Distributor, populated with store name and corporate address, number of stores, contact name, phone number, fax, email. Establish monthly marketing campaign (fax or email)
8. Establish effective method of distribution for E-tailers so product is not always backordered.
9. Contact top industry print magazines for articles
10. Get reviews on websites

DVD Marketing Pull
1. Send screener copy of DVD and one-page description plus artwork to prominent DVD writers, websites, magazines, newspapers for review
2. Reviews/ads on *Film Threat* website among other DVD websites
3. Ads on other websites by trading ad space
4. Niche marketing that is specific to the movie
5. Email marketing with email blasts monthly
6 Message board postings online to spread word
7. Trailer links on official site and other streaming video websites
8. Trade advertising space with other independent films
9. Links to our website from other websites
10. Seek opportunities to spread word direct to fandom

DVD SALES

This step in the process is probably the one that is best delegated to those who excel in sales. The salesman is an entirely, and dramatically, different breed from a filmmaker. If you want proof, just take a look at the shoes. A filmmaker will generally have jeans with perhaps some classic Converse tennis shoes. A salesman has those khaki pants over leather shoes with tassels. These are very different types of people. If it's possible for you to offer a small commission to a salesperson for your DVD, which can be anything from 10% to 30% depending on your terms, I suggest that you do so. The job of sales requires a set of skills foreign to most filmmakers. However, whether you decide to attack the task yourself or hire a salesperson, it is important to understand the basic steps involved in selling a DVD.

First and foremost, manage your expectations when it comes to the number of copies you hope to sell and the money you will potentially make. If you break even selling your movie on DVD — consider that a success. For the most part, the major movie studios break even on their theatrical releases. So, there is no shame in breaking even and if you can make a living doing it, that is a huge success.

KEY RETAIL CUSTOMERS

You must first begin by compiling a list of key customers — the companies that will actually be buying your DVDs. You'll have sales from companies big and small, so create a list of buyers for your title. The chart below is the actual customer list used to sell the DVD *Starwoids*.

DVD DISTRIBUTION KEY CUSTOMER LIST – USA

WHOLESALE	Sales	RETAIL	Sales
Alliance (AEC)	Raleigh	AAFES (Army / Air Force)	Marie
Anchor Bay	Marie	American Stores	Raleigh
Anderson Distribution	Char	Ames	Marie
Arc Distributors	Kim	As Seen On TV Stores	Kim
Arrow Distribution	Marie	Babbage's	Kim
Baker & Taylor	Raleigh	Best Buy	Marie
Electric Fetus	Marie	Blockbuster Corp.	Kim
Flash Distributing	Char	Border's Books	Marie
Gonzales	Raleigh	Circuit City (Ingram)	Char
Image Entertainment	Kim	Consolidated Stores	Char
Ingram Entertainment	Kim	Electronics Boutique	Char
Music City	Raleigh	EURPAC	Raleigh
Music Network	Raleigh	Fred Meyer	Char
Music People	Char	Fry's Electronics	Char
Music Video Distributors (mvd)	Char	Hasting's Books, Music & Video	Marie
Norwalk Distributors	Char	Hollywood Entertainment	Kim
S & J Distributors	Kim	J & R Music	Char
Southwest Wholesale	Raleigh	Kmart (Anchor Bay)	Marie
Unique	Big Al	Leisure Ent.	
Universal One Stop	Marie	Midwest Ent.	
Valley Media	Kim	Movie Gallery (Ingram)	Raleigh
VPD (Video Products Distribution)	Kim	Musicland Entertainment Group	Marie
Wax Works	Raleigh	Music Factory	Raleigh
Wolfe	Char		

RETAIL Cont.	Sales	CATALOG	Sales
Serendipity	Char	Collage Video Catalog	Kim
Southern Stores	Kim	Critics Choice	Marie
Summit Service/Meijers	Marie	Diamond Comics	Kim
Target	Marie	Doubleday Direct	Char
TLA	Char	Library Video	Kim
Tower Records & Video	Char	Movies Unlimited	Char
Transworld (Camelot, Record Town,	Kim	PBS Catalog	Char
Coconuts, Sat. Matinee, Specs, DJ,etc.)		Playboy Catalog	Marie
Virgin Stores	Char	Publisher's Clearing House	Char
Walmart (Anderson)	Char	Reader's Digest	Char
Wherehouse	Char	Rivertown Trading Company	Char
The Wiz	Char		
		CLUB	
INTERNET		Costco	Kim
Amazon.com	Char	B.J.'s Wholesale	Raleigh
Barnes & Noble.com	Char	Sam's Club	Kim
BigStar.com	Char		
Borders.com	Marie		
Buy.com	Marie		
DVD Empire.com	Marie		

CREATIVE MARKETING DRIVES DVD SALES

SOLICITATION — SELLING YOUR DVD

Understand that whether you are distributed by a small DVD publisher or are self-distributing, all major chains buy their titles from a larger distributor. It's the only way to get your foot into stores like Best Buy, Wal-Mart, and Blockbuster. The DVD buyers for those chains simply could not handle the large number of individuals bombarding them to buy titles. The way they buy titles is throuugh catalogs sent to them by large distributors like Ventura. In order to get featured in the catalog and get the attention of buyers from the leading chains carrying DVDs, you must purchase ad space in those catalogs. The cost is reasonable for this exposure, usually just over $1,000.

Your first decision in this process should be your on-sale date. You must backwards engineer your schedule to be sure that your title arrives at the distributor's warehouse in time to meet the chosen on-sale date. In selecting that all-important date, pay attention to fortuitous timing and any other factors which may benefit your film publicity-wise. All your effort should go toward maximum awareness peaking on that day. Additionally, it is critical that the on-sale date be met — otherwise distributors can refuse to receive your DVD and retailers may not place your product on the shelf.

This sample DVD sales release schedule for *Starwoids* illustrates how a schedule might look. This one is very basic, but you can make it as detailed as you like. You might choose to include press events and publicity which coincide with certain milestones in your schedule. (*Please see chart on page 176*).

THE DVD SELL SHEET

The DVD sell sheet is a necessary tool in selling your title to stores. Effectively, the sell sheet is an order form for your movie. One side of the sell sheet should contain all the elements of your DVD sleeve carefully laid out onto a 8 1/2" x 11" sheet of paper. In addition, there will be sales contact information and the UPC code so that retailers who choose to carry your title can simply scan the product code to enter it into their inventory. The sell sheet is a piece of marketing used solely by purchasers of DVDs for stores — not consumers. Therefore the sales sheet is driven to get the attention of

Production Schedule Budget

Title Sleevoids

Due Date	Revised Date	Actual Date	Task	07-Aug	14-Aug	21-Aug	28-Aug	04-Sep	11-Sep	18-Sep	25-Sep	02-Oct	09-Oct	Budget	Supplier	Terms	Due Date	Actual
Artwork:																		
14-Aug			Photos to Artist													Net 60	Nov-01	
21-Aug			Draft Artwork															
28-Aug			Final Artwork															
28-Aug			Filmmaker Approval															
Authoring																		
11-Sep	17-Sep															Net 60	Nov-01	
11-Sep	17-Sep																	
Printing																		
04-Sep	12-Sep		Artwork to Printer													net 30		
25-Sep	18-Sep		DVD Slip Cover															
25-Sep	18-Sep		VHS Slip Cover															
Sales Materials																		
04-Sep	n/a		Draft Sell Sheet Design													n/a		
11-Sep	n/a		Final Sell Sheet Completed															
11-Sep	n/a		Sell Sheet to Printer													net 30		
18-Sep	n/a		Sell Sheet to IndieDVD															
25-Sep	n/a		Sell Sheet delivered to Customers															
Replication																		
18-Sep	22-Sep		Art Materials to Replicator											$7,500	Future Media	net 30		
18-Sep	18-Sep		DLT to Replicator											$2,750	Skura ITC	delivery		
02-Oct	25-Sep		DVD Replication											$400	Future Media (shipping)			
02-Oct	25-Sep		VHS Replication															
02-Oct	25-Sep		DVD Product Ships to Distributor															
02-Oct	25-Sep		VHS Product Ships to Distributor															
03-Oct	26-Sep		DVD Product Arrives at Distributor															
03-Oct	26-Sep		VHS Product Arrives at Distributor															
Order Processing																		
25-Sep	25-Sep		Set Up Pricing / SKU											$280	Ventura	deducted		
11-Sep	11-Sep		Acct Set Up & Approval for all orders															
03-Oct	29-Sep		Ship Initial Orders - Distributors															
06-Oct	01-Oct		Initial Orders Arrive at Distributors															
06-Oct	02-Oct		Ship Initial Orders - Retailers															
09-Oct	08-Oct		Initial Orders Arrive at Retailers															
Street Date																		

Total: $10,900

buyers, not the everyday DVD consumer. This piece of trade marketing does not need to be particularly design intensive, but it must have the following:

- Cover of your DVD
- Synopsis of your movie
- Sales contact info
- On-sale date
- Quotes from press or quotes from reviews
- Highlight notable actors' other work (such as: Stars Wil Wheaton of *Star Trek the Next Generation* and *Stand by Me*)
- Festival awards or accolades
- Elements of your marketing plan (*Planned promotion with major cereal company or contests, advertising you plan to buy, etc.*)
- Any other relevant information pertaining to the potential sales of the title
- UPC code

The flip side of the sell sheet may include a more detailed synopsis of the film or press. It's also wise to include elements of your sales plan to instill confidence in the buyer that your company is heavily supporting the awareness of this title. It is recommended to print these sales sheets, leaving the flip side blank so you can print whatever you would like later. Consider using the sales sheet for trade shows, foreign markets, order forms — this sheet will prove useful for many purposes, so leave one side blank for whatever you need in the future. You may want to use it later for a sales promotion marking down the price of your movie and offering incentives to buyers such as: *Newly priced to sell at $9.99 MSRP plus 1 free T-shirt for every 10 DVDs ordered.*

Also, you'll want to make two versions of your DVD sell sheet — one that is actually printed and the other in PDF format to be sent by email. The electronic version of your sell sheet will come in handy when doing a mass email blast to thousands of privately owned video stores across the country as well as dealing with foreign buyers.

The sample sell sheet reproduced here (*see page 178*) highlights the key selling points for each title. (Note: The front of the sell sheet is always reproduced in color, but for the purposes of this book, you are seeing it in black and white. The flip side containing further information is usually in black and white to save on printing costs.)

UPC CODE

If you are going to self-distribute your movie and get it into the retail marketplace, you must have a UPC code. I do not recommend going to the UPC Code Council and paying their exorbitant fee just so you can output one UPC code. Simply find an outlet online where you can buy a UPC code; it should cost no more than $40. You must have your own unique UPC code for your DVD and it must appear on the back of the sleeve. The best way to decide where it should go is to look at other DVDs as a guide.

PAYMENT TIMELINE

Initially you'll be shocked by how the amount deducted from the cost before the money finally reaches you, the filmmaker. A title sold for $14.99 at retail wholesales at $8.99 (that's 40% off), along with another 20% off the MSRP for the distributor (about $2.99), leaving $5.99 for yourself, not including marketing fees, sales commission, manufacturing costs, or your DVD publisher's take. That leaves only a few dollars of profit left. The math can be worked out so many different ways depending on the MSRP, the deals you make, which tasks are delegated, or how many others share in the profit pie. While the dollars earned per unit will vary greatly, the one thing you can count on is that it will take a long time to get paid. By the time the money reaches you from the customer who bought your title at Best Buy, 120 days or more will have passed. It takes that long for the money to filter back to you. Payment terms are always negotiable, but you often will not be the one in the driver's seat in this scenario, in which case you will be stuck with the distributor's standard terms. And to make matters worse, your title will always be subject to returns — unsold product that is sent back to the distributor for credit against their bill.

It is realistic to expect to see final sales figures for your title within 12 to 18 months. Yes, it will be at least a year. This somewhat depressing reality makes direct sales, those through your own website and to individual video stores, all the more appealing. To understand how the money flows, take a look at this sales payout timeline from a small DVD distributor releasing two titles a month and observe how the revenue is distributed over the course of the calendar year.

DVD Proforma Accounting Statements

Month 1 Activity	Units	Dollars	Statement Balance
Gross Sales	6,000	$ 50,400.00	
customer discounts		$ (2,520.00)	
returns	-	$ -	
net units shipped	6,000	$ 47,880.00	$ 47,880.00
distribution fee		-17.500%	
		$ (8,379.00)	$ 39,501.00
Gross Sales		$ 50,400.00	
reserves (on Gross)		-25%	
		$ (12,600.00)	$ 26,901.00
Co-op Advertising			$ 26,901.00
Misc Deductions			$ 26,901.00
Advances	$	-	$ 26,901.00

Amount due beginning Month 4
Amount credited to account of Month 6 Activity

Month 2 Activity	Units	Dollars	Statement Balance
balance forward			$ -
Gross Sales	7,000	$ 58,800.00	
customer discounts		$ (2,940.00)	
returns	-	$ -	
net units shipped	7,000	$ 55,860.00	$ 55,860.00
distribution fee		-17.500%	
		$ (9,775.50)	$ 46,084.50
Gross Sales		$ 58,800.00	
reserves (on Gross)		-25%	
		$ (14,700.00)	$ 31,384.50
Co-op Advertising	$		$ 31,384.50
Misc Deductions	$	-	$ 31,384.50
Advances	$	-	$ 31,384.50
refurbishing fees	-	$ -	$ 31,384.50
returns fees	-	$ -	$ 31,384.50
drop ship fees	-	$ -	$ 31,384.50
prededuction: Auth Returns		$ (12,600.00)	$ 18,784.50
Credit back prededuction		$	$ 18,784.50

Amount Due beginning of Month 5
Amount credited to account of Month 7 Activity

Month 3 Activity	Units	Dollars	Statement Balance
balance forward			$ -
Gross Sales	7,500	$ 63,000.00	
customer discounts		$ (3,150.00)	
returns	(1,500)	$ (12,600.00)	
net units shipped	6,000	$ 47,250.00	$ 47,250.00
distribution fee		-17.500%	
		$ (8,268.75)	$ 38,981.25
Gross Sales		$ 63,000.00	
reserves (on Gross)		-25%	
		$ (15,750.00)	$ 23,231.25
Co-op Advertising	$	-	$ 23,231.25
Misc Deductions	$	-	$ 23,231.25
Advances	$	-	$ 23,231.25
refurbishing fees	-	$ -	$ 23,231.25
returns fees	-	$ -	$ 23,231.25
drop ship fees	-	$ -	$ 23,231.25
prededuction: Auth Returns		$ (10,080.00)	$ 13,151.25
Credit back prededuction		$ 12,600.00	$ 25,751.25

Amount due beginning of Month 6
Amount credited to account of Month 8 Activity

Month 4	Units	Dollars	Statement Balance
balance forward			$ -
Gross Sales	6,000	$ 50,400.00	
customer discounts		$ (2,520.00)	
returns	(1,200)	$ (10,080.00)	
net units shipped	11,640	$ 37,800.00	$ 37,800.00
distribution fee		-17.500%	
		$ (6,615.00)	$ 31,185.00
Gross Sales		$ 50,400.00	
reserves (on Gross)		-25%	
		$ (12,600.00)	$ 18,585.00
Co-op Advertising	$	-	$ 18,585.00
Misc Deductions	$	-	$ 18,585.00
Advances	$	-	$ 18,585.00
refurbishing fees	-	$ -	$ 18,585.00
returns fees	-	$ -	$ 18,585.00
drop ship fees	-	$ -	$ 18,585.00
Reserve repay		$ -	$ 18,585.00
dist fee on reserve repay		$ (14,280.00)	$ 4,305.00
prededuction: Auth Returns		$ 12,600.00	$ 16,905.00
Credit back prededuction			

Amount due beginning of Month 7
Amount credited to account of Month 9 Activity

Month 5 Activity	Units	Dollars	Statement Balance
balance forward			$ -
Gross Sales	8,500	$ 71,400.00	
customer discounts		$ (3,570.00)	
returns	(1,700)	$ (14,280)	
net units shipped	6,800	$ 53,550.00	$ 53,550.00
distribution fee		-17.500%	
		$ (9,371.25)	$ 44,178.75
Gross Sales		$ 71,400.00	
reserves (on Gross)		-25%	
		$ (17,850.00)	$ 26,328.75
Co-op Advertising	$	-	$ 26,328.75
Misc Deductions	$	-	$ 26,328.75
Advances	$	-	$ 26,328.75
refurbishing fees	-	$ -	$ 26,328.75
returns fees	-	$ -	$ 26,328.75
drop ship fees	-	$ -	$ 26,328.75
Reserve repay		$ -	$ 26,328.75
dist fee on reserve repay		$ (15,120.00)	$ 11,208.75
prededuction: Auth Returns		$ 14,280.00	$ 25,488.75
Credit back prededuction			

Amount due beginning of Month 8
Amount credited to account of Month 10 Activity

Month 6 Activity	Units	Dollars	Statement Balance
balance forward			$ -
Gross Sales	9,000	$ 75,600.00	
customer discounts		$ (3,780.00)	
returns	(1,800)	$ (15,120)	
net units shipped	7,200	$ 56,700.00	$ 56,700.00
distribution fee		-17.500%	
		$ (9,922.50)	$ 46,777.50
Gross Sales		$ 75,600.00	
reserves (on Gross)		-25%	
		$ (18,900.00)	$ 27,877.50
Co-op Advertising	$	-	$ 27,877.50
Misc Deductions	$	-	$ 27,877.50
Advances	$	-	$ 27,877.50
refurbishing fees	-	$ -	$ 27,877.50
returns fees	-	$ -	$ 27,877.50
drop ship fees	-	$ -	$ 27,877.50
Reserve repay		$ 12,600.00	$ 40,477.50
dist fee on reserve repay		$ (3,024.00)	$ 37,453.50
prededuction: Auth Returns	-	$ (15,960.00)	$ 21,493.50
Credit back prededuction		$ 15,120.00	$ 36,613.50

Amount due beginning of Month 9
Amount credited to account of Month 11 Activity

Month 7 Activity	Units	Dollars	Statement Balance
balance forward			$ -
Gross Sales	9,500	$ 79,800.00	
customer discounts		$ (3,990.00)	
returns	(1,900)	$ (15,960)	
net units shipped	11,640	$ 59,850.00	$ 59,850.00
distribution fee		-17.500%	
		$ (10,473.75)	$ 49,376.25
Gross Sales		$ 79,800.00	
reserves (on Gross)		-25%	
		$ (19,950.00)	$ 29,426.25
Co-op Advertising	$	-	$ 29,426.25
Misc Deductions	$	-	$ 29,426.25
Advances	$	-	$ 29,426.25
refurbishing fees	-	$ -	$ 29,426.25
returns fees	-	$ -	$ 29,426.25
drop ship fees	-	$ -	$ 29,426.25
Reserves repay		$ 14,700.00	$ 44,126.25
dist fee on reserve repay		$ (3,528.00)	$ 40,598.25
prededuction: Auth Returns		$ (16,464.00)	$ 24,134.25
Credit back prededuction		$ 15,960.00	$ 40,094.25

Amount due beginning of Month 10
Amount credited to account of Month 12 Activity

Month 8 Activity	Units	Dollars	Statement Balance
balance forward			$ -
Gross Sales	9,800	$ 82,320.00	
customer discounts		$ (4,116.00)	
returns	(1,960)	$ (16,464)	
net units shipped	7,840	$ 61,740.00	$ 61,740.00
distribution fee		-17.500%	
		$ (10,804.50)	$ 50,935.50
Gross Sales		$ 82,320.00	
reserves (on Gross)		-25%	
		$ (20,580.00)	$ 30,355.50
Co-op Advertising	$	-	$ 30,355.50
Misc Deductions	$	-	$ 30,355.50
Advances	$	-	$ 30,355.50
refurbishing fees	-	$ -	$ 30,355.50
returns fees	-	$ -	$ 30,355.50
drop ship fees	-	$ -	$ 30,355.50
Reserves repay		$ 15,750.00	$ 46,105.50
dist fee on reserve repay		$ (3,780.00)	$ 42,325.50
prededuction: Auth Returns		$ (16,800.00)	$ 25,525.50
Credit back prededuction		$ 16,464.00	$ 41,989.50

Amount due beginning of Month 11
Amount credited to account of Month 13 Activity

Month 9 Activity	Units	Dollars	Statement Balance
balance forward			$ -
Gross Sales	10,000	$ 84,000.00	
customer discounts		$ (4,200.00)	
returns	(2,000)	(16,800)	
net units shipped	8,000	$ 63,000.00	$ 63,000.00
distribution fee		-17.500%	
		$ (11,025.00)	$ 51,975.00
Gross Sales		$ 84,000.00	
reserves (on Gross)		-25%	
		$ (21,000.00)	$ 30,975.00
Co-op Advertising		$ -	$ 30,975.00
Misc Deductions		$ -	$ 30,975.00
Advances		$ -	$ 30,975.00
refurbishing fees	-	$ -	$ 30,975.00
returns fees	-	$ -	$ 30,975.00
drop ship fees	-	$ -	$ 30,975.00
Reserves repay		$ 12,800.00	$ 43,575.00
dist fee on reserve repay		$ (3,150.00)	$ 40,425.00
prededuction: Auth Returns		$ (16,800.00)	$ 23,625.00
Credit back prededuction		$ 16,800.00	$ 40,425.00

Amount due beginning of Month 12
Amount credited to account of Month 14 Activity

Month 10 Activity	Units	Dollars	Statement Balance
balance forward			
Gross Sales	10,000	$ 84,000.00	
customer discounts		$ (4,200.00)	
returns	(2,000)	(16,800)	
net units shipped	11,640	$ 63,000.00	$ 63,000.00
distribution fee		-17.500%	
		$ (11,025.00)	$ 51,975.00
Gross Sales		$ 84,000.00	
reserves (on Gross)		-25%	
		$ (21,000.00)	$ 30,975.00
Co-op Advertising		$ -	$ 30,975.00
Misc Deductions		$ -	$ 30,975.00
Advances		$ -	$ 30,975.00
refurbishing fees	-	$ -	$ 30,975.00
returns fees	-	$ -	$ 30,975.00
drop ship fees	-	$ -	$ 30,975.00
Reserve repay		$ 17,850.00	$ 48,825.00
dist fee on reserve repay		$ (4,462.50)	$ 44,362.50
prededuction: Auth Returns		$ (16,800.00)	$ 27,562.50
Credit back prededuction		$ 16,800.00	$ 44,362.50

Amount due beginning of Month 13
Amount credited to account of Month 15 Activity

Month 11 Activity	Units	Dollars	Statement Balance
balance forward			$ 30,975.00
Gross Sales	10,000	$ 84,000.00	
customer discounts		$ (4,200.00)	
returns	(2,000)	(16,800)	
net units shipped	8,000	$ 63,000.00	$ 93,975.00
distribution fee		-17.500%	
		$ (11,025.00)	$ 82,950.00
Gross Sales		$ 84,000.00	
reserves (on Gross)		-25%	
		$ (21,000.00)	$ 61,950.00
Co-op Advertising		$ -	$ 61,950.00
Misc Deductions		$ -	$ 61,950.00
Advances		$ -	$ 61,950.00
refurbishing fees	-	$ -	$ 61,950.00
returns fees	-	$ -	$ 61,950.00
drop ship fees	-	$ -	$ 61,950.00
Reserve repay		$ 18,900.00	$ 80,850.00
dist fee on reserve repay		$ (4,536.00)	$ 76,314.00
prededuction: Auth Returns		$ (13,104.00)	$ 63,210.00
Credit back prededuction		$ 16,800.00	$ 80,010.00

Amount due beginning of Month 14
Amount credited to account of Month 16 Activity

Month 12 Activity	Units	Dollars	Statement Balance
balance forward			$ -
Gross Sales	7,800	$ 65,520.00	
customer discounts		$ (3,276.00)	
returns	(1,560)	(13,104)	
net units shipped	6,240	$ 49,140.00	$ 49,140.00
distribution fee		-17.500%	
		$ (8,599.50)	$ 40,540.50
Gross Sales		$ 65,520.00	
reserves (on Gross)		-25%	
		$ (16,380.00)	$ 24,160.50
Co-op Advertising		$ -	$ 24,160.50
Misc Deductions		$ -	$ 24,160.50
Advances		$ -	$ 24,160.50
refurbishing fees	-	$ -	$ 24,160.50
returns fees	-	$ -	$ 24,160.50
drop ship fees	-	$ -	$ 24,160.50
Reserve repay		$ 19,950.00	$ 44,110.50
dist fee on reserve repay		$ (4,788.00)	$ 39,322.50
prededuction: Auth Returns		$ (12,000.00)	$ 27,322.50
Credit back prededuction		$ 13,104.00	$ 40,426.50

Amount due beginning of Month 15
Amount credited to account of Month 17 Activity

FULFILLMENT AND SHIPPING

Whenever you see "shipping and handling" attached to any order for a product, that means that someone is being paid to fulfill your order. You may choose to personally keep all your DVDs in your garage or basement or living room and personally mail out DVDs, but your time is better spent on your next movie. It's more efficient to hire a fulfillment house to ship DVDs for you and you can find one near you by using *google.com*. Just be sure to pass along those shipping and handling costs to those ordering your DVD.

ONLINE SALES

There are two places where you will be selling your DVD online — one is to various online stores like Amazon.com and Netflix and the other is through your own official website. Sales through your website will offer you the best profit margin — but it may cost more in the long run since you will have to reach out to potential customers with advertising. To maximize sales from your own store, offer some kind of incentive that the customer will receive *only* if they purchase the DVD from the official shop. Incentives might include:

- ▸ Signed and numbered copy of the DVD
- ▸ Free poster
- ▸ Free T-shirt
- ▸ Free button
- ▸ Bonus DVD

Whatever incentive you offer, if it costs only a few dollars, you will still make more money from that sale than you will selling at your wholesale price to other online outlets. It is recommended to sell on Amazon.com. They will either get your DVD from a distributor, or you can sell through their Advantage Program. The upside is that Amazon has such a large regular customer base. It's the difference between having a store in the shady part of town (your website) and having an outlet in a large shopping center or mall where everyone shops (Amazon). You might consider holding back release for 90 days while you sell your DVD exclusively at your online shop — that way you will get the bulk of the initial orders while you also collect positive reviews. Then, after that three-month period, sell to as many other online stores as will carry your title. That way you've squeezed as many direct sales of your title as possible.

See the appendix in the back for a list of online sales outlets.

FOREIGN DVD SALES

To capitalize on foreign sales of your DVD, you need to hire a qualified sales rep well versed in the market desires of each territory. A foreign sales agent will generally get a 20% commission from the sale, so if you sell to a country like Thailand for $2,000, you're going to end up with a check for $1,600 minus the cost of the duplicate master (which is about $200), for a net return of about $1,400. Now that kind of money does not sound like a lot, but there are more than 80 viable territories that you could sell to, so the money can add up quickly if your movie becomes hot. The actual price paid will vary greatly and your sales agent will know the ins and outs of what buyers are looking for in each territory and what they are willing to pay.

This is something that I do not recommend that you attempt on your own. Look carefully at your contract and be aware that when you sell your rights to a certain territory, you are often selling *all* rights to that territory, including television, cable, DVD, and video. Additionally, your foreign sales agent may recommend selling your film as part of a library or package of films to increase the number of territories in which it could be sold. Ask your rep how many other films he is repping and if yours will be bundled with other movies. Sometimes this can be a good thing and it helps you to be aware of how your film is being sold.

It's also important to be prepared to have your DVD deliverables ready for possible sales. You must have:

▸ DVD disc art
▸ DVD sleeve art
▸ English-language transcription of your film
▸ Master copy of your movie, textless, with the music, effects, and dialogue on separate tracks

The master should have the music and effects on one track with the dialogue on a second track so that whichever foreign territory picks it up, they can decide if they want to dub or subtitle your movie. By having a transcript, it will be easy for them to translate it. The buyer will also specify the tape format for delivery. Having all these materials ready and waiting is going to make it that much easier to close a deal. One piece of advice: Get cash up front for any deal. There are many unscrupulous people in this arena, so be careful going into any deal.

INCREASE FOREIGN SALES WITH SUBTITLES

Subtitling your movie on a budget is not very difficult. My own film *Red* is subtitled in ten different languages, including Chinese and Japanese. When foreign buyers express interest in purchasing the rights to your film, already having your movie subtitled dramatically increases the chances that you will close a deal with a buyer from that territory. Additionally, by having English-language subtitles, your film will be suitable for viewing by the hearing impaired. It is worth the time to subtitle your movie if only to open up as many opportunities as possible for sales. The more potential customers, the better.

Earlier, we explained how to do this technically. The first step is to create a transcript of all the words spoken in the film along with any signs or text relevant to the story. Once you have this transcript, visit a website like *www.freetranslation.com* and, by cutting and pasting portions of the text, you will have your film translated into many different languages. (One word of warning: The translation is not perfect, so your subtitles may sound silly to native speakers. Think *Austin Powers*.) You'll need to clean up the copy a little bit. Having subtitles in various foreign languages is a distinct advantage when closing deals for foreign territories.

TEN INSIDER SECRETS FOR SELLING YOUR DVD

Here are some final words of advice from leaders in the independent DVD world who offer their own keys to success.

1. **Advertise in both trade and consumer publications.** "Advertising makes an enormous difference, possibly the difference between selling 10,000 units and 100,000 units," says Troma chief Lloyd Kaufman. "So make sure you have money in your budget to place ads for distributor magazines, film magazines or circulars."

2. **Budget accordingly.** "Don't make a $50,000 movie and spend another $50,000 in DVD authoring because you may not make it back," comments Don May of Synapse Films. "A good number to keep in mind is to tell yourself you are only going to sell about 5,000–10,000 units total. Budget with that in mind."

3. **Great photos make great marketing materials.** "Still photography is very important during the making of a film," says Tanya York of York Entertainment, "since this is where art campaigns are born. Many times producers leave photography as an afterthought, which makes it very difficult to then market the film later." Jonah Loeb of Indie DVD agrees, "Take production stills, have a day of photos with the actors taking good shots for the poster/video box/glosses. It's not all about getting it in the camera." Loeb feels cover art is critical. "Focus the majority of your attention on your packaging, it is the single most important sales piece," he says.

4. Shop for DVD pricing. "Shop around for the best DVD mastering price," reiterates Don May. "You'll be surprised at the different programs many DVD pressing plants may offer." May adds, "When pricing and estimating your sales numbers, keep in mind that many distributors won't want to buy it unless you give them 50 – 60% off your retail price."

5. Grassroots and guerilla marketing. While the benefits of a promotional website are obvious, "Both the DVD and the site must be pushed relentlessly," says Troma chief Lloyd Kaufman. "Troma owes much to its grassroots campaigns of having fans spread the word on the web through emails and posts."

6. Embrace extras that sell. Jonah Loeb stresses the need to add special content that will sell instead of rent. "Add something to the DVD that helps the consumer cross the threshold of 'should I buy it or rent it?'" Loeb also points out, "It also helps if you can add something that is so unique it inspires reviews, word of mouth, and general viewing pleasure. There is so much more that you can add with a DVD that, frankly, independent film needs to get its foot in the door." However, May of Synapse Films thinks that DVDs can go too far when it comes to extras. "Don't go overboard with the extras if you think your movie is going to be a hard sell," he says. "Sure, some extras are fine, but adding hours of material for a title that many distributors may not even know about isn't going to help."

7. Distributor relations are critical. "Never expect every distributor to pay utmost attention to all your titles in the same way," May divulges. "Make sure that your distributors are really pushing it to their full potential. Give them incentives, give them a list of selling points and ideas." Loeb agrees and urges, "Begin selling your title at least 90 days before release, buyers are looking at films way early which is a disadvantage to independents who go out of pocket on production even earlier than they would normally like to."

8. Competitors can be allies. "Make friends out of fellow small competitors," encourages Loeb. "The odds are too great against you to operate in a vacuum."

9. Timing is key. Jonah Loeb stresses the importance of "connecting your film in some way to major releases. Find the hook of your film and follow the lead of the most successful similar release." Indie DVD's release of the

Kevin Smith executive-produced title *Drawing Flies* also benefited from the same week release of *Jay and Silent Bob Strike Back.*

10. Involve the filmmakers. "Add special features that tell the story of the filmmaker," says Loeb. "A good success story can only add to the film." He also encourages filmmakers to deliver the highest quality end product. "Sound is two-thirds of your film, write that down in preproduction." Don May encourages the filmmaker's involvement at every step. "Make sure to approve everything with the film's producers." Yet he adds, "And never expect to get rich in this business."

Final Track

We've detailed the processes required to design a high-quality DVD which can compete aggressively against major releases. The skills involved in producing your title are very similar to the skills you used to make your film. As we've also discussed, the steps necessary to effectively market your title are very similar to those involved in promoting your film on the festival circuit.

Even sales, while a specialized talent, is something you know how to do — you had to *sell* your idea to a financier, you had to *sell* your actors on playing the part, and you had to *sell* your crew on your creative vision to inspire them to make your independent movie. In other words, you already possess many, if not most, of the abilities needed to release your film on DVD. Our goal is to explain how to apply those abilities to your DVD project.

We've tried to clearly spell out each phase in the production of a DVD in an effort to demystify this process and put the tools for success into your hands. We've presented methods that are known to work when partnered with a formidable creative vision. Lessons learned from the artistic battles you fought to make your film a reality will be put to good use throughout the course of your DVD production. Finishing the film was difficult enough; now comes the next step in your filmmaking career.

Since we've been there ourselves, we know it's not easy, so we sincerely wish you luck along the way. Congratulations on getting your film made. Now get it out there.

Section 6

APPENDIX
DVD
RESOURCES

SAMPLE DVD DISC ART

SAMPLE DVD MENU ARCHITECTURE FOR THE MOVIE *RED*

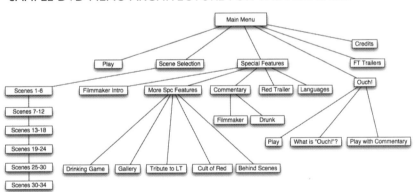

SAMPLE DVD MENU DESIGN – ROUGH

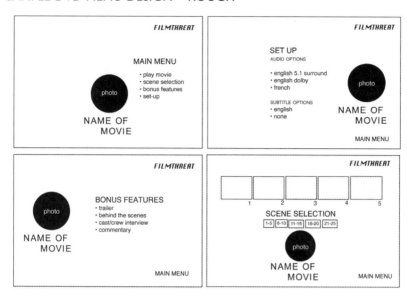

SAMPLE DVD MENU DESIGN – COMPLETE

SAMPLE DVD SLEEVE

DVD PRODUCTION STEPS

The following overview of suggested DVD production steps will help you schedule the release of your DVD. From concept to completion, it can take as little as six weeks to produce a high-quality DVD or as long as six months or more. By assigning deadlines to the following tasks, you can begin to plan the production of your project.

Prepping
- ▸ Sign distribution deal or choose to self-distribute
- ▸ Collect assets
- ▸ Plan and schedule
- ▸ Conceive ideal DVD
- ▸ Organize assets

Authoring and Production
- ▸ Create a flowchart
- ▸ Create a bit budget

- Prepare video assets
- Prepare audio assets
- Create menus
- Import assets
- Author the DVD
- Test the DVD
- Output a DLT master
- Deliver DLT master and artwork to replication facility

Marketing
- Build your marketing plan
- Map out strategy to address the following elements:
- Packaging
- Publicity, Press and Promotion
- Reviews
- Advertising
- Timing
- Create impactful packaging to be used for sales
- Send early review copies to critics to gather quotes
- Seek out champion for film
- Book advertising to coincide with release date
- Build press release list and send out initial release
- Plan other promotions and contests

Sales
- Determine on-sale date
- List title for sale on online stores
- Announce release date for DVD
- Create sell sheet
- Contact independent video stores
- Deal with distributor
- Mail sell sheet to buyers
- Follow up with buyers
- Continue to solicit buyers with incentives
- Email blast and online promotion
- Web promotion ongoing

DVD PRESS RELEASE FORMAT

FOR IMMEDIATE RELEASE
DATE
Contact: Name
Contact number or email
[HEADLINE – Something catchy]
[Sub-Headline; more informative than "attention"- grabbing headline]
[CITY] – Your DVD company announces the release of [DVD Title] by [Filmmaker]. This special edition DVD contains extra features [DVD specs].

[Paragraph description of DVD Title: synopsis, filmmaker tidbits, about 500 words total]
[DVD Title] carries a [Price] SRP and is available direct from your DVD company or from fine retailers everywhere. Check for stores in your area at *www.yourfilmwebsite.com*

About the Production Company
A short blurb about the production company, especially if you have made other films.

About the Filmmaker
Include a short bio here, about 100 to 200 words.

For screener copies of the DVD, contact:
The best way to reach you including your address, phone number, and email address.

DVD Production Services

This portion of the book is not meant to provide a complete directory; these resource listings merely act as a starting point for your own research. It's up to you to do the legwork necessary in order to get the best pricing for the services you seek. Always check online for the most up-to-date contact info as well as other sources.

Abet Disc Plus
1833 Casa Grande St.
Pasadena, CA 91104
tony@abetdisc.com
www.abetdisc.com
T: 626-791-4114 F: 626-791-3163
Services: DVD authoring, DVD-5, -9 and -10 replication, short-run DVD-Rs, Amaray case insert printing and packaging.

Accord Productions
2140 South Dixie Hwy. #301
Miami, FL 33133
max@accordvideo.com
www.accordvideo.com
T: 305-856-1245 F: 305-856-9101
Services: DVD mastering (PAL and NTSC), authoring, PAL conversion, duplication, replication.
Equipment/System Offered: Sonic Solutions encoding and mastering.

Action Duplication, Inc.
8 Union Hill Rd.
West Conshohocken, PA 19428
jlevitt@actionduplication.com
www.actionduplication.com
T: 800-828-7580 F: 610-828-7401

Services: Two full-service DVD authoring Suites, replication and packaging. DVD-R duplication; serial digital input to DVD encoders, on-disc digital printing.
Equipment/System Offered: DVD Authoring on Spruce Maestro and Composer System.

Advanced Media Post
4001 W. Magnolia Blvd
Burbank, CA 90505
alesh@ampost.com
www.ampost.com
T: 818-973-1660 F: 818-973-1669
Services: Menu design, compression and authoring, project management, stereo and surround sound design/editing, video editing, recording studio, value added production, print graphics design.
Equipment/System Offered: Digital Vision Bitpack Studio Encoding, Pinnacle Cinewave Final Cut Pro video/audio editing, Pro Tools, Scenarist Authoring, Motion Menu rendering workstations.

AGI Media
5055 Wilshire Blvd.
Los Angeles, CA 90036
www.agimedia.com
T: 323-937-0220
Services: Unique DVD packaging solutions
for the entertainment industry.

Allied Vaughn
7951 Computer Avenue S.
Minneapolis, MN 55435
cindy.verant@alliedvaughn.com
www.alliedvaughn.com
T: 800-323-0281 F: 952-832-3179
Services: DVD duplication, replication,
authoring, encoding, packaging, and graphic
design, distribution and media on-demand.

Americ Disc Inc.
2525 Canadien
Drummondville, PQ J2C7W2
info@americdisc.com
www.americdisc.com
T: 819-474-2655 F: 819-478-4575
Services: Mastering, replication, print,
packaging, fulfillment, returns processing,
copy protection.

B1Media
11846 Ventura Blvd., Suite 300
Studio City, CA 91604
b1@b1media.com
www.b1media.com
T: 818-755-8800 F: 818-755-8818
Services: DVD authoring, interactive design,
DVD-ROM.

Blink Digital
545 Fifth Ave., 2nd Fl.
New York, NY 10017
info@blinkdigital.com
www.blinkdigital.com
T: 212-661-6900 F: 212-907-1233

Services: Menu design, compression and
authoring, project management, surround
sound mixing, bonus feature production.
Equipment/System Offered: Motion design
stations, broadcast Sony Encoder, Scenarist
authoring, Pro Tools HD.

Carpel Video, Inc.
429 East Patrick St.
Frederick, MD 21701
Acarpel@carpelvideo.com
www.carpelvideo.com
T: 800-238-4300
Services: DVD authoring, DVD duplication,
transfer other formats to DVD, editing
video, video duplication.
Equipment/System Offered: DVDit!

CD Digital Card
Rancho Cucamonga, CA USA
Mohab Sabry, Vice President
sabry@cddigitalcard.com
www.cddigitalcard.com
T: 800-268-1256 F: 909-481-7307

Cdigital Markets, Inc.
Baltimore, MD USA
Tom Booth, Jr., Vice President, Sales
tbooth@secmedia.com
www.cdigitalmarkets.com
F: 410-646-7786

Cdman Disc Inc.
4794 West 6th Ave., Vancouver, BC
info@cdman.com
www.cdman.com
T: 800-557-3347 F: 604-261-3313
Services: Accepts DVD-R as master (no DLT
needed), full-service DVD-5, -9 and -10
replication, graphic design, packaging.
Equipment/System Offered: mastering, full
replication services.

Chace Productions
201 S.Victory Blvd.
Burbank, CA 91502
audio@chace.com
www.chace.com
T: 800-842-8346 F: 818-842-8353
Services: Sound restoration and remastering
for DVD. Specialists in converting mono
into 5.1/6.1 stereo. Audio compression and
AC-3 and DTS encoding.
Equipment/System Offered: Sonic Solutions
NoNoise, Cube-Tec Audio Cube, Chace Digital
Stereo Processor, THX® pm3 certified mixing.

**Cine Magnetics Video & Digital
Laboratories**
100 Business Park Dr.
Armonk, NY 10504
cminfo@cinemagnetics.com
www.cinemagnetics.com
T: 800-431-1102 F: 914-273-7575
Services: Authoring, replication, and
distribution. Foreign-language dubbing and
subtitling, custom package design and
printing, warehouse and distribution services,
800-number inbound order capturing,
credit card processing and e-commerce
integration services.

Cinram, Inc.
4905 Moores Mill Rd.
Huntsville, AL 35811
sales@cinram.com
www.cinram.com
T: 800-433-3472 F: 256-852-8706
Services: Copy protection, mastering services,
replication, distribution, packaging, project
management.

Cloud Nineteen
3757 Overland Ave., #104
Los Angeles, CA 90034
www.cloud19.com

T: 310-839-5400 F: 310-839-5404
Services: DVD authoring and design,
packaging design, and duplication services.

Comchoice
1025 W. 190th St., Ste. 200
Gardena, CA 90248
sales@comchoice.com
http://www.comchoice.com
T: 310-630-1360 F: 310-630-1365
Services: Turnkey DVD and CD-ROM
production services; concepting and storyboarding; authoring, encoding and
interactive programming; motion menus;
3D/Flash animation; sound design; video
post production; graphic design; packaging
and replication; front-end Web design;
development of electronic press kits.
Equipment Offered: Proprietary Toshiba
authoring, proprietary online project
management application, proprietary assets
management application, encoding and
emulation, Pro Tools, Final Cut, Avid,
Motion Design Stations.

Crawford Communications, Inc.
3845 Pleasantdale Rd.
Atlanta, GA 30340-4205
chip.stephenson@crawford.com
www.crawford.com
T: 404-876-7149, 800-831-8027
F: 678-421-6717
Services: Turnkey projects and individual
services such as; DVD authoring and
compression; MPEG-1 and MPEG-2
compression; CBR or VBR; 5.1 Dolby s
urround sound; custom authoring and
custom menus in both NTSC and PAL;
output to either DVD-R or DLT.
Equipment/System Offered: Sonic Creator
system with 5.1 surround sound.

Creative Domain
6922 Hollywood Blvd., 7th Fl.
Hollywood, CA 90028
mitchellr@creativedomain.com
www.creativedomain.com
T: 310-845-3000 F: 310-845-3030
Services: Interface design, set-top game
design, DVD-ROM development. Added-
value production, authoring and encoding.

Crest National
Digital Media Concepts
6721 Romaine St.
Hollywood, CA 90038
info@crestnational.com
www.crestnational.com
T: 323-860-1314 F: 323-466-7128
Services: Complete menu graphic design;
VBR MPEG-2 encoding; Dolby T digital &
DTS multichannel audio encoding, mono
through full surround; PCM capture &
MPEG Layer II encoding; complete
authoring and QC disc emulation services.
DVD manufacturing capabilities include
mastering, replication, printing and
packaging services for DVD-9, -5 and -10.

DaTARIUS Technologies, Inc,
15-A Marconi Avenue
Irvine, CA 92618 USA
americas@datarius.com
T: 949-452-9211 F: 949-452-9214

Deluxe Media Services, Inc.
200 S. Flower St.
Burbank, CA 91502
Natalie.Kinsey@byDeluxe.com
www.bydeluxe.com
T: 818-525-2100 F: 818-525-2101
Services: DVD mastering, replication,
packaging, fulfillment, distribution.

Denon Digital LLC
Madison, GA USA
Brian Wilson, President & COO
bwilson@denondigital.com
www.denondigital.com
F: 706-342-3537

Denon Digital LLC
New York, NY USA
Ric Sherman, Vice President, National Sales
rsherman@denondigital.com
www.denondigital.com
F: 646-282-3301

Devlin Video International
1501 Broadway, Ste. 408
New York, NY 10036
cdavis@devlinvideo.com
www.devlinvideo.com
T: 212-391-1313 F: 212-391-2744
Services: DVD authoring, disc design,
video preparation, audio preparation,
menu creation, subpicture creation,
layout, proofing and premastering.
Equipment/System Offered: Creator
and Scenarist software.

Disc Makers
Pennsauken, NJ USA
David Olinsky, National Sales Director
info@discmakers.com
www.discmakers.com
T: 800-468-9353 F:856-661-3450
Services: Disc Makers offers a complete
service for the audio CD and CD-ROM
buyer who needs small quantities (300 up).

Disc USA
Plano, TX USA
Thomas L. Groshans, Sales Manager
thomasg@discusa.com
www.discusa.com
T: 800-929-8100 F: 972-509-0694

DISCFARM Corporation
Corona, CA USA
Charlie Chien, President
info@discfarm.com
www.discfarm.com
F: 909-279-4038

Echodata Group
Coatesville, PA USA
Stephen Roberts, CEO
sroberts@echodata.com
www.echodata.com
F: 610-466-2110

Eclipse Data Technologies
Pleasanton, CA USA
Bob Edmonds, VP Sales & Marketing
sales@eclipsedata.com
www.eclipsedata.com
F: 925-224-8881
Services: Eclipse is a leading developer of
DVD and CD mastering encoders and
software, providing leading edge capability
with a reputation for technical excellence
and world-class customer support.

Flex Products Inc.
Santa Rosa, CA USA
Jon Noce, East Coast Sales Manager
john_noce@flexpro.com
www.secureshift.com
F: 978-465-5942

Future Media Productions
Valencia, CA USA
Dave Moss, Vice President
dmoss@fmpi.com
www.fmpi.com
F: 661-294-5582
Services: Since 1994, Future Media
Productions, located in Valencia, California,

has grown to be the largest independent
CD/DVD replication plant on the West
Coast and offers replication services for all
major CD and DVD formats.

Graphland, Inc.
Los Angeles, CA USA
Zareh Aghajanian, Vice President
zareh@graphland.com
www.graphland.com
T: 888-545-8655 F: 323-454-4301

Henninger Media Services
2601-A Wilson Blvd.
Arlington, VA 22201
TMCcarthy@henninger.com
www.henninger.com
T: 703-243-3444 F: 703-522-3933
Services: Authoring DVD-V, DVD-Audio,
DVD-Rom, VBR video compression, motion
graphic menu creation, project management, concept and design, MLP, DTS, Dolby
Digital 5.1 + Stereo, MPEG-2 and PCM
audio encoding, music composition, surround
audio design and mixing, duplication,
translation services and QC. HD video
production and post production, telecine,
linear and non-linear HD editing.
Equipment/System Offered: Sonic Creator
and Spruce Maestro.

HI FI Media Replicators, Inc.
Studio City, CA USA
Frank Liva, President
info@mediareplicators.com
www.mediareplicators.com
F: 818-752-9284

Imperial Tape Company, Inc.
1928 14th St.
Santa Monica, CA 90404
info@nutunes.com
www.nutunes.com
T: 310-396-2008 F: 310-396-8894
Services: Duplication, replication, DVD
packaging, authoring, mastering.

InfoDisc
Culver City, CA USA
S.W. Park, President Ron Robins, Vice
President Sales & Marketing
ron_robins@infodiscusa.com
www.infodiscusa.com
F: 310-280-1222
Services: Your Single Source Solution,
Worldwide, for DVD, CD, VHS
replication/duplication, packaging
and distribution.

Inoveris
Dublin, OH USA
Melodie Gee, Vice President & General
Manager, Content Delivery
gee@metatec.com
www.metatec.com
F: 614-718-4580

I.V.I. International Video Innovation
20879 Plummer St.
Chatsworth, CA 91311
Guy Lavy
T: 818-718-1965 F: 818-700-9020
Services: Duplication, replication, DVD
packaging, authoring, mastering.

Jaync
1232 17th Ave. South
Nashville, TN 37212
info@jaync.com
www.jaync.com

T: 615-320-5050 F: 615-340-9559
Services: authoring, video encoding,
surround mixing, mastering, surround
sound design, audio editing, video editing,
Dolby Digital encoding, DTS encoding,
MLP encoding.
Equipment/System Offered: Sonic Solutions,
Minnetonka Chrome, Pro Tools with AV
Option XL, Final Cut Pro.

JVC Disc America Company
Los Angeles, CA USA
Sean Smith, Sr. VP - Sales & Marketing
Tom Kenney, National Accounts Executive
www.jvcdiscusa.com
F: 310-274-4392

Krauss-Maffei Optical Disc
3845 E Coronado Street
Anaheim, CA 92807
Christian Rath
crath@krauss-maffeicorp.com
T: 714-575-0018 F: 714-575-9277

LA Studios
3453 Cahuenga West
Hollywood, CA 90068
www.lastudios.com
T: 323-851-6351(Facility) / 323-497-2240
F: 323-876-5347
Services: DVD after-session duplication
and spot authoring.

LaserPacific Media Corporation
809 N. Cahuenga Blvd.
Hollywood, CA 90038-3703
jthill@laserpacific.com
www.laserpacific.com
T: 323-462-6266 F: 323-960-2134
Services: Film laboratory, complete post-
production services, authoring, encoding,
menu design, MPEG-1 and -2, HD MPEG,

fiber & digital connectivity.
Equipment Offered: State-of-the-art
proprietary system.

Margarita Mix de Santa Monica
1661 Lincoln Blvd.
Santa Monica, CA 90404
www.lastudios.com
T: 310-396-3333; 323-497-2240
F: 310-396-9633
Services: DVD after-session duplication
and spot authoring.

Margarita Mix Hollywood
6838 Romaine Street
Hollywood, CA 90038
www.lastudios.com
T: 323-497-2240; 323-962-6565
F: 310-962-6662

Masterdisk Studios
545 W. 45th St.
New York, NY 10036
info@masterdisk.com
www.masterdisk.com
T: 212-541-5022 F: 212-265-5645
Services offered: DVD concept and
design, DVD-Video and -Audio
creative development.

Maxwell Productions, LLC
8521 E. Princess Dr.
Scottsdale, AZ 85255
info@maxwellproductions.com
www.maxwellproductions.com
T: 480-627-1000
Services: Glass mastering, replication DVD
& CD, printing, packaging.

Metropolis DVD
88 10th Ave. Ste. 6W
New York, NY 10011
info@metropolisdvd.com
www.metropolisdvd.com
T: 212-675-7300 F: 212-765-9336
Services: Menu design, compression and
authoring, project management, DVD-R
duplication surround sound mixing, bonus
feature production and editing.
Equipment Offered: Motion design stations,
broadcast Sony encoder, Scenarist and
Creator authoring, Pro Tools HD,
uncompressed video editing suite.

Midtown Video
4824 S.W. 74 Court
Miami, FL 33155
rheslop@midtownvideo.com
jwheeler@midtownvideo.com
www.midtownvideo.com
T: 305-669-1117 F: 305-662-2860
Services: Sell Apple & Sonic Solutions
software and sell Rimage Corporation
DVD replication and mass customization
solutions. Midtown Video also sells and
rents Broadcast & Professional video
and audio equipment.
Equipment/System Offered: Apple, Sonic
Solutions and Rimage Corporation.

Nexpak
6370 Wise Ave., NW
North Canton, OH 44720
sales@nexpak.com
www.nexpak.com
T: 800-442-5742 F: 330-490-2011
Services: Packaging products and services for
DVD and DVD-Audio formats for a wide
array of content providers including studios,
replicators and retail organizations. Our

innovative solutions range from our specialty packaging like the WYNcase with a paperboard cover and crystal-clear trays to our standard Amaray case.

NowDisc
875 W. McGregor Ct., Suite 100
Boise, ID 83705
info@nowdisc.com
www.nowdisc.com
T: 208-388-0249
Services: DVD duplication

Philips DVD +RW
PO Box 80002, 5000 JB
Eindhoven, The Netherlands
Niels Leibbrandt
n.leibbrandt@philips.com
www.dvdrw.com
T: +31 40 2735614

Philips Super Audio CD
PO Box 80002, 5000 JB
Eindhoven, The Netherlands
Matthijs Peters
matthijs.peters@philips.com
www.superaudiocd.philips.com
T: +31 402 738978

R-Quest Technologies, LLC
1012 McHenry Ave
Modesto, CA 95350
info@r-quest.com
www.r-quest.com
T: (Toll Free) 877-4R-QUEST (477-8379)
T: (Direct) 209-522-8700

ScreamDVD
333 7th Ave., 10th Fl.
New York, NY 10001
info@screamdvd.com
www.screamdvd.com

T: 212-951-7171 F: 212-629-8009
Services: PAL/NTSC encoding, DVD authoring, finalization to DLT, DVD-R check discs, replication, complete emulation and testing.

SF Video, Inc.
1548 Stockton St., 2nd Fl.
San Francisco, CA 94118
steven@sfvideo.com
www.sfvideo.com
T: 415-288-9400 F: 415-288-9410
Services: DVD replication, printing, packaging, and fulfillment. Minimum DVD orders 2,000 units per title. Also VHS duplication/CD replication.

Sony Precision Technology America
20381 Hermana Circle
Lake Forest, CA 92630
barnak@spt.sony.com
www.spt.sony.com
T: 949-770-8400 F: 949-770-8408
Equipment/System Offered: DEC-10 & -11 DVD ECC Checkers (versions for bonded and unbonded discs).

speeDVD Co.
17145 Rinaldi St.
Granada Hills, CA 91344
customerservice@speedvd.com
www.speedvd.com
T: 818-368-3210 F: 818-368-6117
Services: Complete DVD compression/ authoring services including static & motion/sound menu design/creation. Equipment/System Offered: Spruce Maestro System include. MPX3000 (C-Cube) Encoder, NTSC: DV-Cam, BetaSP, Digi-Beta, PAL: Digi-Beta, DA-98/DA-98HR: 16- or 24-bit Multichannel Digital Audio, DTS and Dolby Digital Surround Sound Encoding, DVD-R and DLT deliverables.

Stancon Video
569 King St. East, Ontario
info@stanconvideo.com
www.stanconvideo.com
T: 416-360-3933 F: 416-360-1755
Services: Professional DVD authoring
(Highest-end system available). Video
encoding from any professional format,
5.1 digital audio encoding, package design,
title and menu design, end-to-end DVD
project implementation, closed caption
and subtitling for DVD.
Equipment/System Offered: DBeta, BetaSP,
D1, D2, MiniDV, DVCam, 3/4", MPEG1,
MPEG2, MPEG4, AVI, WMF, QuickTime.

Surround Associates
11333 Ventura Blvd.
Studio City, CA 91604
bobbyo@surroundassociates.com
www.surroundassociates.com
T: 818-487-9298 F: 818-487-9229
Services: 5.1 audio services for DVD -Video,
DVD -Audio, and SACD including full
multitrack and stem remixing, mono and
stereo to 5.1 upmixing (exclusive
representatives for the FDS process), Dolby
Digital and DTS encoding, VCD and ECD
creation, extra element production
(commentary tracks, two- and three-camera
shoots for interviews), graphic design,
authoring, production management,
surround audio consultation (studio setup
and calibration), live event recording for DVD.
Equipment/System Offered: Three multi-
million-dollar, purpose-built 5.1 audio studios
equipped with Euphonix S5, CS-3000 and
SSL-9000 consoles, Pro Tools, Nuendo,
Euphonix R-1, three custom 5.1 editing bays.

Technicolor
3233 E. Mission Oaks Blvd.
Camarillo, CA 93012
info@technicolor.com
www.technicolor.com
T: 805-445-1122 F: 805-445-4340
Services: authoring, compression, mastering,
DVD replication, CD replication, VHS
duplication, disc printing, packaging,
fulfillment, storage, returns processing.

The Pod Studios
12872 Valley View St., Studio 1
Garden Grove, CA 92845
rhorine@thepod.tv
www.thepod.tv
T: 714-799-6911, 888-5-thepod
F: 714-799-6912
Services: Complete audio/video production,
broadcast, DVD, packaging and print design,
motion graphics and animation; audio and
video editing, compositing, encoding,
authoring, subtitles, closed captioning,
international formats, web links, PC extras,
special features, merchandising tie-ins,
restoration, print and replication management,
VOD, IFE in-flight lab services.

The Victory Studios
2247 15th Ave. West, Seattle, WA 98119
11755 Victory Blvd.
North Hollywood, CA 91606
matt@victorystudios.com
www.victorystudios.com
T: 888-282-1176 F: 206-282-3535
Services: Basic DVD, authored DVD, two-
pass VBR MPEG-2 encoding, duplication,
replication, support for DVD-R authoring,
DVD-R general and DVD+R Media, DLT
output.
Equipment/System Offered: Sonic Scenarist,
Sony Vizaro, Sonic Creator.

TopKopy
12 Skyline Dr.
Hawthorne, NY 10532
bsaliani@topkopy.com
www.topkopy.com
T: 914-345-2650 F: 914-345-2617
Services: authoring, duplication.

Unaxis
18881 Von Karman Ave., Suite 200
Tower 17 Irvine CA 92612
Helfried Weinzerl
Unaxis Data Storage
helfried.weinzerl@unaxis.com
T: 949-863-1857 F: 949-863-1866

Video Arts, Inc.
724 Battery St.
San Francisco, CA 94111
ksalyer@vidarts.com
www.vidarts.com
T: 415-788-0300 F: 415-788-3331
Services: Menu design, DVD authoring,
MPEG-2 encoding, AC-3 encoding,
navigation design, and project consulting.
Equipment/System Offered: Sonic Solutions
DVD Creator authoring system, Minerva
hardware encoder, Sonic SD-2000 encoder,
Apple DVD Studio Pro, Digital Rapids
hardware encoder, Heuris MPEG encoder,
Spruce Virtuoso authoring.

Visual Sound, Inc.
937 N. Citrus Ave.
Hollywood, CA 90038
Craig Pepe/Charley Brooks
cpepe@visualsoundinc.com
www.visualsoundinc.com
T: 323-962-5990 F: 323-962-5992

WAM!NET
10900 Hampshire Ave. South
Bloomington, MN 55438
Tom Van Sickle
tomv@savvis.net
www.wamnet.com
T: 952-852-4882 F: 952-852-4808

DVD Authoring Software

Recommended software for authoring
DVDs:

DVD Studio Pro - Apple

iDVD - Apple

DVDit! - Sonic Solutions

Encore - Adobe

Impression - Pinnacle Systems

DVD Packaging Services

Ace Packaging Incorporated
153 West Rosecrans Avenue
Gardena, CA 90248
V. Jun Flores
vjflores@ace-cases.com
www.ace-cases.com
T: 310-225-6658

AGI Media
299 Park Ave., 12th Floor
New York, NY 10171
Richard Roth
EVP, Sales and Marketing
richard.roth@agimedia.com
www.agimedia.com
T: 212-318-5643

ART Entertainment
711 East Wardlow Road
Long Beach, CA 90807
Lyle Einstein
leinstein@rocktenn.com
T: 562-997-0100

Auriga Aurex Inc.
Ann Arbour, MI USA
Ellie Remar, Regional Sales Manager
ellieremar@comcast.net
F: 734-971-2939

Bert-Co
1855 Glendale Blvd.
Los Angeles, CA 90026
Heather Swedlund
info@bertco.com
T: 323-669-5877 F: 323-669-5850

Carthuplas, Inc.
7 Shape Drive
Kennebunk, ME 04043
Betsy Winstead
Vice President of Sales
bwinstead@carthuplas.com
www.carthuplas.be
T: 207-985-4972

CD Digital Card
Rancho Cucamonga, CA USA
Mohab Sabry, Vice President
sabry@cddigitalcard.com
www.cddigitalcard.com
T: 800-268-1256 F: 909-481-7307

Cdigital Markets, Inc.
Baltimore, MD USA
Tom Booth, Jr., Vice President, Sales
tbooth@secmedia.com
www.cdigitalmarkets.com
F: 410-646-7786

Cinram, Inc.
4905 Moores Mill Rd.
Huntsville, AL 35811
sales@cinram.com
www.cinram.com
T: 800-433-3472 F: 256-852-8706

Clear Vu Products
29 New York Ave.
Westbury, NY 11590
Grace Consoli
gconsoli@clear-vu.com
T: 800-221-4545 x 120
F: 516-333-8880 x 120

Deluxe Media Services, Inc.
200 S. Flower St.
Burbank, CA 91502
Natalie.Kinsey@byDeluxe.com
www.bydeluxe.com
T: 818-525-2100 F: 818-525-2101

Disc Makers - LA
Los Angeles, CA USA
John Moyer, Sales Manager
info@discmakers.com
T: 800-731-8009 F: 323-876-6724

Disc Makers - NJ
Pennsauken, NJ USA
David Olinsky, National Sales Director
info@discmakers.com
www.discmakers.com
T: 800-468-9353 F: 856-661-3450

Disc Makers - NY
New York, NY USA
Jeff Epstein, Sales Manager
info@discmakers.com
www.discmakers.com
T: 800-446-3470 F: 212-352-0573

Disc USA
Plano, TX USA
Thomas L. Groshans, Sales Manager
thomasg@discusa.com
www.discusa.com
T: 800-929-8100 F: 972-509-0694

DISCFARM Corporation
Corona, CA USA
Charlie Chien, President
info@discfarm.com
www.discfarm.com
F: 909-279-4038

DuPont - DuPont Tyvek®
Chestnut Run Plaza, Bldg. 728/3204
4417 Lancaster Pike
Wilmington, DE 19805
Michael P. Buri
Senior Marketing Communications Specialist
Michael.P.Buri@usa.dupont.com
www.discpackaging.tyvek.com
T: 302-999-3886 F: 302-999-4135

Echodata Group
Coatesville, PA USA
Stephen Roberts, CEO
sroberts@echodata.com
www.echodata.com
F: 610-466-2110

EMI Music Distribution
Jacksonville, IL USA
Tom Peterson, National Sales Manager
tom.peterson@emicap.com
www.emimfg.com
T: 888-616-0600 F: 217-587-9202

GIMA Advanced Technology Inc.
38 N. Lively Blvd.
Elk Grove, Illinois 60007
Gary Helfrecht

infous@gima.com
www.gima.com
T: 847-952-9329 F: 847-952-9382

Graphland, Inc.
Los Angeles, CA USA
Zareh Aghajanian, Vice President
zareh@graphland.com
www.graphland.com
T: 888-545-8655 F: 323-454-4301

Inoveris
Dublin, OH USA
Melodie Gee, Vice President & General Manager, Content Delivery
gee@metatec.com
www.metatec.com
F: 614-718-4580

International Packaging Corp.
Fort Wayne, IN USA
Pete Costello, President & COO
ipc@natplastics.com
www.internationalpkg.com
F: 260-482-8941

Kyoto America
670 Hardwick Road Unit #2, Bolton
Ontario, Canada L7E 5R5
Peter Wardell
sales@kyotoamerica.com
www.kyotoamerica.com
T: 905-951-2727 F: 905-951-1221

Ross-Ellis Packaging Solutions
8300, Tampa No. J
Northridge, CA 91325
Nina Palmer
National Sales Manager
palmern@transcontinental.ca
www.ross-ellis.com
T: 800-447-2149 F: 818-993-4760

Saati Americas
247 Route 100
Somers, NY 10589
Frank Basch
Product Portfolio Manager
info.US@saatiprint.com
www.marabu.com
T: 914-232-7781 or 800-431-2200
F: 914-232-4004

Sagoma Technologies
16 Landry Street
Biddeford, ME
Tatiana Gelardi or Tony Gelardi
admin@sagomaplastics.com
www.sagomaplastics.com
T: 207-284-1772 F: 207-284-7616

Scanavo Ltd.
5512 4th Street N.W.
P. O. Box 64153
Calgary, Alberta, Canada T2K 6J1
Kim Sorensen, President
sales@scanavo-ltd.com
www.scanavo.com
T: 403-250-6855 F: 403-250-6844

Shorewood Packaging
277 Park Avenue, 30th floor
New York, NY 10172-3000
Ken Rosenblum, Sr. V.P., Home
Entertainment Sales
shorewoodpackaging@ipaper.com
www.shorewoodpackaging.com
T: 212-371-1500

Super Jewel Box USA
1537 W. Collins Avenue
Orange, CA 92867
Andrew Schuurs,
VP/GM
info-usa@superjewelbox.com

www.superjewelbox.com
T: 866-4-SJB-USA or 714-288-8960
F: 714-288-8967

Univenture
4707 Roberts Road
Columbus, OH 43228
David Coho
Director of Sales
sales@univenture.com
www.univenture.com
T: 614-529-2100 or 800-992-8262
F: 614-529-2110

White Tiger Media
351-G Electronics Blvd.
Huntsville, AL 35824
Brad Johnson
www.whitetigeronline.com
T: 888-682-5333 or 256-704-5333
F: 256-319-0202

National Distributors

These distributors fulfill titles to national
retailers across the country.

Alliance Entertainment Group
http://www.aent.com/

Ingram Entertainment
http://www.ingramentertainment.com

Baker and Taylor
http://www.btol.com

Video Products Distributors, Inc.
http://www.vpdinc.com/html/vpd_profile.htm

Independent DVD Distributors

The following is a brief list of DVD distributors; inclusion in this list is by no means an endorsement of any of kind. Since often multiple addresses and contact info is provided on each website, we've provided the website for each so you can easily obtain the latest contact information. Be sure to research each distributor's specialty to find the right match for your film. There are distributors specializing in dramas, foreign, horror, sci-fi, exploitation, animation, art film, gay-themed, documentaries, comedies, urban, ethnic, music, family film and religious movies, so be sure to pursue one that matches your film.

AI Multimedia
www.ai-multimedia.com

Alternative Cinema
www.alternativecinema.com

Anchor Bay
www.anchorbayentertainment.com

Ardustry
www.anchorbayentertainment.com

Asylum
www.theasylum.cc/home.html

Barrel Entertainment
www.barrel-entertainment.com

BijouFlix Releasing
www.bijoucafe.com

Blue Underground
www.blue-underground.com

Brain Damage Fil
www.braindamagefil.com

CAV
www.cavd.com

Cloud Ten
www.cloudtenpictures.com

Cult Epics
www.cultepics.com

CutthroatVideo
www.cultepics.com

Department 13
www.dept13.com

Direct Video
www.directvideo.com

Eclectic DVD
www.eclecticdvd.com

E. I. Independent Cinema/Seduction
Cinema/Shock-O-Rama
www.eicinema.com

Elite Entertainment
www.elitedisc.com

Englewood Entertainment
www.englewd.com

Facets Multimedia, Inc.
www.facets.org

Film Threat DVD
www.FilmThreatDVD.com

First Look Pictures
www.flp.com

First Run
www.firstrunfeatures.com

Fox
www.foxhome.com

Grapevine Video
www.grapevinevideo.com

Heretic Fil
www.hereticfil.com

Home Vision/Criterion
www.homevision.com

Image Entertainment
www.image-entertainment.com

Kino
www.kino.com

Koch Entertainment
www.kochint.com

Leo Fil
www.leofil.com

Lions Gate
www.lionsgatefil.com

Media Blasters
www.media-blasters.com

Milestone Film & Video, Inc.
www.milestonefil.com

Movies Unlimited
www.moviesunlimited.com

MPI Home Video
www.mpimedia.com

MTI/Fangoria/Bedford/Artist View
www.mtivideo.com

Music Video Distributors (MVD)
www.musicvideodistributors.com

New Concorde
www.newconcorde.com

New Line
www.newline.com

New Yorker Video
www.newyorkerfil.com

Retromedia
www.retromedia.org

ScreenEdge
www.screenedge.com

Sinister Cinema
www.sinistercinema.com

Slingshot Entertainment
www.slingshotent.com

Sony Pictures
www.sonypictures.com/homevideo

Sub Rosa
www.b-movie.com

Synapse Fil
www.synapse-fil.com

Tai Seng
www.taiseng.com

TLA Video
www.tlavideo.com

Troma
www.troma.com

Universal
www.homevideo.universalstudios.com

Urban Vision
www.urban-vision.com

Vanguard International Cinema
www.lainet.com/vanguard/index.htm

Ventura Distribution
www.venturadistribution.com

VCI
www.vcihomevideo.com

Wild East
www.wildeast.net

Wolfe Video
www.wolfevideo.com

World Artists
www.worldartists.com

York Entertainment
www.yorkentertainment.com

Zeitgeist Film
www.zeitgeistfilm.com

Zia Film
www.ziafilm.com

DVD Online Rental

Café DVD
www.cafedvd.com

DVD Avenue
www.dvdavenue.com

DVD Overnight.com
www.dvdovernight.com

GreenCine
www.greencine.com

Mercury DVD
1-877-823-3396
www.mercurydvd.com

Netflix
www.netflix.com

QwikFliks.com
www.qwikfliks.com

Independent Video Stores in U.S. and Canada

The following is a short list of independently owned video stores that may be approached directly for sales of your DVD title. It is recommended to contact them by email and ask to speak directly to the store manager in charge of purchasing new titles.

ALBUQUERQUE
Alphaville Video
3408 Central SE
Albuquerque, NM
505-256-8243
info@alphavillevideo.com

ALEXANDRIA
Video Vault
323 S. Washington St.
Alexandria, VA 22314
800-VAULT-66
jim@videovault.com

ANCHORAGE
Bosco's Comics, Cards & Games
2606 Spenard Rd.
Anchorage, Alaska 99503
907-274-4112
orders@boscos.com
mailorders@boscos.com

AUSTIN
I Luv Video
info@iluvvideo.com

Pedazo Chunk Video
2009 South First St.
Austin, TX 78704
512-441-3505
dannie@pedazochunk.com
pedazochunk@pedazochunk.com

Vulcan Video (2 stores)
info@vulcanvideo.com

Video Station Superstore
800 Mallard Ln.
Taylor, TX 76574
512-365-6474
video@videostation.net

Waterloo Video
1016 W. 16th St.
Austin, TX 78703
512-474-2525
video@waterloorecords.com

BALTIMORE
Bigg Wolf Movie Discounters
9421 Georgia Ave.
Silver Spring, MD 20910
877-587-9333
biggwolf@erols.com

BOSTON
Cinemasmith
Ken Hastings, Mgr.
283 Harvard St.
Brookline, MA 02446
617-232-6637
Kenhas@cinemasmith.net

Hollywood Express Video (4 stores)
George Lewis
1740 Massachusetts Ave.
Cambridge, MA 02138
617-868-5533
info@hollywoodexpressvideo.com

The Video Underground
Attn: Yvonne
389 Centre St.
Jamaica Plain, MA 02130
617-522-4949
thevideounderground@yahoo.com

CINCINNATI

Wizard's Music & Movies
Oakley Square
2940 Markbreit Ave.
Cincinnati, OH 45209
513-351-5500
info@wizardsmusicandmovies.com

DENVER

Cheap Discs
Cheapo@cheapodiscs.com

HOUSTON

Cactus Music and Video
Attn: Kristina
2930 S. Shepard
Houston, TX 77098
713-526-9272
cactusmusicandvideo@yahoo.com

Major League Video
(3 stores)
majorleaguevideo@yahoo.com

LOS ANGELES

Video Annex
Mike Smith
4533 MacArthur Blvd., #186

Newport Beach, CA 92660
Videoannex@onebox.com

Alpha and Omega Movies
214-890-0260
alphaomegamovies@yahoo.com

Cinefile Video
11280 Santa Monica Blvd.
Los Angeles, CA 90025
310-312-8836
info@cinefilevideo.com

Fastlane Video
12726 Hadley St., #102
Whittier, CA 90601
562-698-3313

Laser Blazer
10587 West Pico Blvd.
LA, CA 90064
310-475-4788
shop@laserblazer.com
listmanager@laserblazer.com

LOUISVILLE

Wild and Woolly Video
Attn: Todd
1021 Bardstown Rd.
Louisville, KY 40204
502-473-0969
wandw@iglou.com

MEMPHIS

Video Magic
Comments@videomagic.com

MIAMI

Lambda Passages Bookstore
7545 Biscayne Blvd.
Miami, FL
Lambdapassages@yahoo.com

Lion Video (2 stores)
305-442-6080
info@lionvideo.com

Tate's Comics+Toys+Videos+More
Tate Ottati
4566 N. University Dr.
Lauderhill, FL 33351
954-748-0181
emailus@tatescomics.com

NEW YORK
Norman's Sound & Vision (8/23)
67 Cooper Square
NY, NY 10003
212-473-6599
normansv@aol.com

The Video Room
(2 stores)
Attn: Howard
212-879-5333 or 212-962-6400
info@videoroom.net
www.videoroom.net

Kim's Video
212-995-0220
Attn: Michael
Michael@kimsvideo.com
Help@kimsvideo.com

OKLAHOMA CITY
Atomik Pop (2 stores)
Steve
Steve@atomikpop.com

ORLANDO
Sci-Fi City
6006 East Colonial Dr.
Orlando, FL 32822
407-282-2292
webdev@sci-fi-city.com

PHILADELPHIA
Movie Mania
Webmaster@moviem.com

PITTSBURGH
Copacetic Comics
1505 Asbury
Pittsburgh, PA 15217
412-422-1344
query@copcomco.com

Dreaming Ant
4525 Liberty Ave.
Bloomfield, PA
412-683-7326
info@dreamingant.com

Eides Entertainment
1121 Penn Ave.
Pittsburgh, PA 15222
412-261-0900
eides@eides.com

Heads Together Video & DVD
Attn: Donna
2127 Murray Ave.
Pittsburgh, PA 15217
412-521-3700
donna.sias@worldnet.att.net
info@headstogether.com

PORTLAND
Curt's Cash Corner
7979 SE Foster Rd.
Portland, OR
503-777-7147

Excalibur Books & Comics
2444 SE Hawthorner Blvd.
Portland, OR 97214
503-231-7351
info@excaliburcomics.net

Mike Clark's Movie Madness
4320 S.E. Belmont
Portland, OR 97215
503-234-4363
mikeclarksmoviemadness@hotmail.com

SAN DIEGO
Movies 2 Sell
Eric J. LaRowe
P.O. Box 17549
San Diego, CA 92177
4724 Clairemont Mesa Blvd.
San Diego, CA 92177
858-274-3020
sales@movies2sell.com

Kensington Video
Attn: Guy
4067 Adams Ave.
San Diego, CA 92116
619-584-7725
kenvideo@cox.net

SAN FRANCISCO
Choi's Home Video
1410 Lombard St.
San Francisco, CA 94124
415-441-5610
choi@choisvideo.com

Dr. Video (2 stores)
Attn: Melinda
1521 18th St.
San Francisco, CA 94107
415-826-2900
anyone@drvid.com

Green Cine
Attn: Jonathan Marlow
537 Stevenson St., Ste. 200
San Francisco, CA 94103
Marlow@greencine.com
content@greencine.com

Le Video
1231 9th Ave.
San Francisco, CA 94122
415-566-3606
www.levideo.com

SAN JOSE
LaserLand Home Theater
1080 South De Anza Blvd.
San Jose, CA 95129
408-253-3733
info@laserlandhometheater.com

Belmont Video and Laser
580 Masonic Way
Belmont, CA 94002
650-594-1808
Bcleopard@Astreet.com

SEATTLE
Scarecrow Video
Attn: Mark
5030 Roosevelt Way NE
Seattle, WA 98105
206-524-8554
mark@scarecrow.com
www.scarecrow.com

ST. LOUIS
Game Force Games CDs & DVDs
10501 Watson Rd.
Sunset Hills, MO 63127
314-966-3900
vgforce@swbell.net

Record Exchange
5320 Hampton Ave.
St. Louis, MO 63109
314-832-2249
contact@recordexchangestl.com
requests@recordexchangestl.com

TORONTO
Suspect Video
Luis Ceriz
416-504-9116
suspectvideo@sympatico.ca

TUCSON
Casa Video
2905 E. Speedway
Tucson, AZ 85716
520-326-6314
info@casavideo.com

R-Galaxy
2420 N. Campbell Ave.
Tucson, AZ 85719
520-322-0422
r-galaxy@r-galaxy.com

TULSA
Gardner's Used Books & Comics
4421 S. Mingo Road
Tulsa, OK 74146
918-627-7323
info@gardnersbooks.com
order@gardnersbooks.com

House of Video
(5 stores)
webmaster@houseofvideo.com

WASHINGTON, DC
Potomac Video (5 stores)
Pvideo@potomacvideo.com

DVD Online Resources

Film Threat DVD
www.FilmThreatDVD.com

IRMA Online Source Directory
www.recordingmedia.org/sourceoutput.cfm

Medialine
www.medialinenews.com/dvd.shtml

Video Software Dealer's Association
www.vsda.org

DVD Reviewers and Media Outlets

This is by no means a complete list, but this directory of freelance writers and media outlets are friendly when it comes to reviewing independent DVDs. Some mainstream outlets are also included on this list, but it always helps to check the submission policy of each media outlet when seeking a review of your DVD. It is also helpful to find a critic who is receptive to the genre of film you are submitting for review.

Jim Neibaur
1220 William Street
Racine, WI 53402

Dennis Schwartz
Ozus' World Movie Reviews
568 Houran Road
Bennington, VT 05201

Michael B. Scrutchin
Flipside Movies Emporium
2707 Glencullen Ln.
Pearland, TX 77584

Michael Gingold
Fangoria
475 Park Avenue South, 8th Floor
New York, NY 10016

Jill Bernstein, Video/DVD Editor
Premiere Magazine
1633 Broadway
New York, NY 10019-6708

Jennifer Hillner
Wired Magazine, "Play" Section
520 Third Street, 3rd Floor
San Francisco, CA 94107-1815

Mike Bracken
CultureDose.net
2694 75th Avenue
Oakland, CA 94605

Sophie Redditt
Have Fun at the Movies
10717 Bushire Drive
Dallas, TX 75229-5330

Kevin Filipski
21 Devine Street
Lynbrook, NY 11563

Nathan Shumate
Cold Fusion Video
1468 N. 350 West
Sunset, UT 84015

Donna Larcen
Hartford Courant
285 Broad Street
Hartford, CT 06115

Jack Wilkinson
1016 Wildwood Road NE
Atlanta, GA 30306

Heather Willis
Pulse!
2500 Del Monte St., Bldg C
W. Sacramento, CA 95691

Barb Vancheri
Pittsburgh Post-Gazette
34 Blvd. of the Allies
Pittsburgh, PA 15222

Doug Nye
The State
P.O. Box 1333
Columbia, SC 29202-1333

Mark Rahner
Seattle Times
1120 John Street
Seattle, WA 98109

Rich Ryan
Staten Island Advance
950 Fingerboard Road
Staten Island, NY 10305

Eric Campos
FilmThreat.com
5042 Wilshire Blvd. PMB 1500
Los Angeles, CA 90036 USA

Mark Harris
Entertainment Weekly
1675 Broadway
New York, NY 10019

Mike Pearson
3226 South Forest Street
Denver, CO 80222

Eileen Fitzpatrick
Billboard
5055 Wilshire Blvd.
Los Angeles, CA 90036-4306

Mike Clark
USA Today
7950 Jones Branch Drive
McLean, VA 22108-0001

Dennis Dermody
455 Hudson Street
New York, NY 10014

Tom Russo
Boston Globe
135 Morrisey Blvd.
Boston, MA 02107

Holly Wagner
Video Store Magazine
201 East Sandpointe Ave., #600
Santa Ana, CA 92707

Heather Lejewski
Chicago Tribune
435 North Michigan Avenue
Chicago, IL 60611-4022

Donald Liebenson
Baker & Taylor
7000 N. Austin Avenue
Niles, IL 60714-4602

Scott Haah
554 West 50th Street
New York, NY 10019-7023

Jessica Wolf
Video Store Magazine
201 East Sandpointe Ave., #600
Santa Ana, CA 92707

Stephanie Prange
Video Store Magazine
201 East Sandpointe Ave., #600
Santa Ana, CA 92707

Brendan Howard
Video Store Magazine
201 East Sandpointe Ave., #600
Santa Ana, CA 92707

Laurence Lerman
Video Business
360 Park Avenue South
New York, NY 10010-1710

Susan King
Los Angeles Times
Times Mirror Square
Los Angeles, CA 90053-3836

Darren Gross, Assistant Editor
VideoHound DVD Guide
1450 N. Vista St., # 101
Los Angeles, CA 90046-4228

Mark Engle
CultCuts Webzine
13742–12th Ave S.W., #94
Seattle, WA 98166

Brian Thomas
6438 N. Hamilton Ave.
Chicago, IL 60645-5608

Home Video Editor
Entertainment News Calendar
250 West 57th Street, #1431
New York, NY 10017

David Germain
Associated Press
221 S. Figueroa, #300
Los Angeles, CA 90012-2553

Tim Lucas
Video Watchdog
P.O. Box 5283
Cincinatti, OH 45205-0283

Ethan LaCroix
Time Out New York
475 Tenth Avenue, 12th Floor
New York, NY 10018

Paul Malcolm
L.A. Weekly
6715 Sunset Blvd.
Los Angeles, CA 90028

Joe Kane
Videoscope
77 Franklin Avenue
Ocean Grove, NJ 07756

Bette-Lee Fox, Video Editor
Library Journal
360 Park Avenue South
New York, NY 10010-1710

Phyllis Levi Mandell, Video Ed.
Library Journal
360 Park Avenue South
New York, NY 10010-1710

John Cochran
Video Mania
175 West 79th St., #11C
New York, NY 10024

Steve Murray
Atlanta Journal-Constitution
72 Marietta Street
Atlanta, GA 30303

Jim Lahm
Video Specialist Newsletter
1025 Stanford Avenue
Fullerton, CA 92831-2809

Duane Dudek
Milwaukee Journal-Sentinel
918 North 4th Street
Milwaukee, WI 53203-1506

John A Douglas
Grand Rapids Press
155 Michigan NW
Grand Rapids, MI 49503

Michael Janusonis
Providence Journal-Bulletin
75 Fountain Street
Providence, RI 02902

Tracy Fisher
Video Store Magazine
201 East Sandpointe Ave., #600
Santa Ana, CA 92707

News Editor
Hollywood News Calendar
15030 Ventura Blvd., #742
Sherman Oaks, CA 91403

Michael J. Weldon
Psychotronic Magazine
4102 Main Street
Chincoteague Island, VA 23336-2408

Randy Pitman
Video Librarian
8705 Honeycomb Court NW
Seabeck, WA 98380-9734

Ted Okuda
1604 W. Berwyn #1
Chicago, IL 60640-2049

Joseph Gelmis
Twilight Park
Cottage 21, Santa Cruz Rd.
Haines Falls, NY 12436

John Rezek
Playboy
680 North Lakeshore Drive
Chicago, IL 60611

Paul Sherman
284 Ferry Street
Malden, MA 02148

Jon M. Gibson
Maximum Play
10061 Riverside Drive, #884
Toluca Lake, CA 91602

Meg Bozzone
Creative Classroom
149 Fifth Avenue, 12th Floor
New York, NY 10010

Jack Garner
61 Beverly Street
Rochester, NY 14610

Gerri Taylor
Booklist
50 E Huron St.
Chicago, IL 60611

Beverly Goldberg
American Libraries, c/o Source
50 E. Huron St.
Chicago, IL 60611

Peter Stack
San Francisco Chronicle
901 Mission Street
San Francisco, CA 94103-2988

Randy Myers
Contra Costa Times
P. O. Box 5088
Walnut Creek, CA 94598-2513

Mark Burger
Winston-Salem Journal
P. O. Box 3159
Winston-Salem, NC 27102-3159

Jeffrey P. Faoro
Alternative Cinema
P. O. Box 371
Glenwood, NJ 07418

Joe Bob Briggs
532 LaGuardia Place, #113
New York, NY 10012

Richard Valley
Scarlet Street
P. O. Box 604
Glen Rock, NJ 07452-0604

Nell Minow
The Movie Mom
4102 North River Street
McLean, VA 22101

Steve Puchalski
Shock Cinema
P. O. Box 518
Peter Stuyvesant Station
New York, NY 10009

Dave Yount
Video Eyeball
291 Western Avenue
Sherborn, MA 01770-1211

Jason Pankoke
MICRO-FILM
P. O. Box 45
Champaign, IL 61824-0045

Harley Lond
OnVideo
9190 West Olympic, #271
Beverly Hills, CA 90212

Scott Tobias
The Onion
47 West Division Street, #385
Chicago, IL 60610

John Salazar, Fast Forward
Entertainment Today
2325 W. Victory Blvd.
Burbank, CA 91506

Steve Hedgpeth, Home Video
The Star-Ledger
1 Star-Ledger Plaza
Newark, NJ 07102

Julie Washington
The Plain Dealer
1801 Superior Avenue E.
Cleveland, OH 44114-2198

Steve Bloom, High Five
High Times
235 Park Avenue South, 5th Floor
New York, NY 10003-1405

Gavin Smith
Film Comment
70 Lincoln Center Plaza
New York, NY 10023-6595

James J. J. Wilson
Outre
P. O. Box 1900
Evanston, IL 60204

Tony Timpone
Fangoria
475 Park Avenue South
New York, NY 10016

Sean Axmaker
"On Video" @ IMDB
5528 E. Greenlake Way North
Seattle, WA 98103

Mike Mayo
Visible Ink Press
291 Hillside Avenue
Chatham, NJ 07928

Joe Meyers
Connecticut Post
410 State Street
Bridgeport, CT 06604-4560

Jeremy Wallace
Burialpark.net
107 Center Pointe Drive
Crystal City, MO 63019

Denis Sheehan
Askew Reviews
P. O. Box 684
Hanover, MA 02339

Nathaniel Thompson
c/o Image Entertainment
9333 Oso Avenue
Chatsworth CA 91311

Allen Richards
c/o www.B-Independent.com
181 Boyer Lane
Berryville, VA 22611

Dwight Kemper
P. O. Box 1094
Vestal, NY 13851-1094

Leo Charney
All-Movie Guide
301 E. Liberty Street
Ann Arbor, MI 48104

Christopher Thompson
About.com
P. O. Box 34246
Detroit, MI 48234-0246

John Beifuss
Commercial Appeal
495 Union Avenue
Memphis, TN 38103-3217

Scott Taylor
1012 2nd Street, #4
Santa Monica, CA 90403

Jackson Casey
Stumped?
P. O. Box 3488
Oak Park, IL 60303-3488

Gary Morris
Bright Lights Film Journal
929 SE 34th Avenue
Portland, OR 97214

Suzanne Hodges
Widescreen Review
26864 Mandelieu Drive
Murrieta, CA 92562

Bob Pardue
DVD Spotlight
115 Chesterfield Highway
Cheraw, SC 29520

Van T. Tran
DVDMG.com
5008 27th Avenue S.
Seattle, WA 98108

Doug Pratt
DVDLaser.com
3510 Riverside Drive
Oceanside, NY 11572

Catherine Applefield Olson
Billboard – Home Video
622 Oakley Place
Alexandria, VA 22302-3611

Nancy Churnin
Dallas Morning News
P. O. Box 655237
Dallas, TX 75265-5237

Rochelle O'Gorman-Flynn
Top Hill Farm
Devon Road
Lee, MA 01238

About the Authors

CHRIS GORE is a writer, filmmaker, and television commentator who has built a solid reputation as an outspoken voice in the independent film world. He was named one of the 25 Most Influential People in Independent Film by *Film Festival Today* magazine.

Chris is widely known as the hilariously honest, down-to-earth creator and editor of the website *Film Threat*. In 2002 he launched a Film Threat DVD distribution label to promote indie films that he felt deserved to be seen by wider audiences. Chris has written for *The New York Times, Alternative Cinema, Total Movie, Blender, Details,* and trade publications such as *Variety, Video Business,* and *The Hollywood Reporter.* He is also the host of the Independent Film Channel original series *Ultimate Film Fanatic* and can be seen regularly on IFC.

Chris began his independent filmmaking career with the cult short *Red* starring Lawrence Tierney. Chris recently shifted his focus to making films such as the World War II action/drama *Straight Into Darkness* and the feature comedy *My Big Fat Independent Movie,* where he also served as the film's producer and co-screenwriter.

Chris lives in Los Angeles with his family and his collection of over 1,000 DVDs. His home on the web can be found at *www.ChrisGore.com.*

Other books by Chris Gore
The Ultimate Film Festival Survival Guide (Lone Eagle Books)
The 50 Greatest Movies Never Made (St. Martin's Press)

About the Authors

PAUL J. SALAMOFF has found simultaneous success as a DVD author/producer, special f/x make-up artist, screenwriter, producer, and director. Born in Natick, Massachusetts, he was raised on a healthy diet of science fiction and horror from the age of five. After high school, he moved to Southern California where he parlayed his obsession for genre filmmaking into a successful run as a professional make-up f/x artist. In 14 years, he has worked on over 40 films, 10 television series, and numerous commercials.

His screenwriting credits include *The Dead Hate the Living*, *The St. Francisville Experiment*, and *Alien Siege* for the Sci-Fi Channel. He also wrote and directed *Unbakeable*, a parody of M. Night Shyamalan's *Unbreakable*, starring Orlando Jones. Currently he is adapting his screenplay *The Silent Planet* into four hardcover graphic novels for Humanoids Inc., as well as developing screenplays for a number of production companies.

Paul runs his own full-service DVD company for which he has produced and authored DVDs for Film Threat and the Insane Clown Posse's Psychopathic Records. He has also served as a segment producer on a number of DVD titles including *Buffy, The Vampire Slayer*, seasons 4 and 5.

Paul lives in Burbank with his wife Melissa (an interior designer), daughter Samantha (a toddler), and his cat Banshee (a brown-mackerel tabby).

You make the MOVIE.
We do the SELLING.

If you use what you learned from this book to promote your movie, you're going to be overwhelmed with orders.

We process all your orders and ship your DVD to your fans the same day so you can focus on making your next film.

You get a check in the mail EVERY WEEK for your sales. We are 100% non-exclusive and hassle free. No uploading, no digitizing. We do it all for you.

TO LEARN MORE or START SELLING, VISIT:
filmbaby.com/member

Indies delivered to your doorstep

877-FILMBABY // filmbaby@filmbaby.com

THE WRITER'S JOURNEY
2ND EDITION
MYTHIC STRUCTURE FOR WRITERS

CHRISTOPHER VOGLER

BEST SELLER
OVER 116,500 UNITS SOLD!

See why this book has become an international bestseller and a true classic. *The Writer's Journey* explores the powerful relationship between mythology and storytelling in a clear, concise style that's made it required reading for movie executives, screenwriters, playwrights, scholars, and fans of pop culture all over the world.

Both fiction and nonfiction writers will discover a set of useful myth-inspired storytelling paradigms (i.e., "The Hero's Journey") and step-by-step guidelines to plot and character development. Based on the work of Joseph Campbell, *The Writer's Journey* is a must for all writers interested in further developing their craft.

The updated and revised second edition provides new insights and observations from Vogler's ongoing work on mythology's influence on stories, movies, and man himself.

"This book is like having the smartest person in the story meeting come home with you and whisper what to do in your ear as you write a screenplay. Insight for insight, step for step, Chris Vogler takes us through the process of connecting theme to story and making a script come alive."

> — Lynda Obst, Producer
> Sleepless in Seattle, How to Lose a Guy in 10 Days
> *Author*, Hello, He Lied

"This is a book about the stories we write, and perhaps more importantly, the stories we live. It is the most influential work I have yet encountered on the art, nature, and the very purpose of storytelling."

> — Bruce Joel Rubin, Screenwriter
> Stuart Little 2, Deep Impact, Ghost, Jacob's Ladder

CHRISTOPHER VOGLER, a top Hollywood story consultant and development executive, has worked on such high-grossing feature films as *The Lion King*, *The Thin Red Line*, *Fight Club*, and *Beauty and the Beast*. He conducts writing workshops around the globe.

$24.95 | 325 PAGES | ORDER # 98RLS | ISBN: 0-941188-70-1

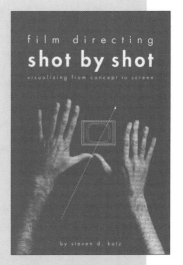

SETTING UP YOUR SHOTS
GREAT CAMERA MOVES EVERY FILMMAKER SHOULD KNOW

JEREMY VINEYARD

BEST SELLER
OVER 27,300 UNITS SOLD!

Written in straightforward, non-technical language and laid out in a nonlinear format with self-contained chapters for quick, on-the-set reference, *Setting Up Your Shots* is like a Swiss army knife for filmmakers! Using examples from over 140 popular films, this book provides detailed descriptions of more than 100 camera setups, angles, and techniques — in an easy-to-use horizontal "wide-screen" format.

Setting Up Your Shots is an excellent primer for beginning filmmakers and students of film theory, as well as a handy guide for working filmmakers. If you are a director, a storyboard artist, or an animator, use this book. It is the culmination of hundreds of hours of research.

Contains 150 references to the great shots from your favorite films, including *2001: A Space Odyssey*, *Blue Velvet*, *The Matrix*, *The Usual Suspects*, and *Vertigo*.

"Perfect for any film enthusiast looking for the secrets behind creating film. Because of its simplicity of design and straightforward storyboards, Setting Up Your Shots *is destined to be mandatory reading at film schools throughout the world."*
— Ross Otterman, Directed By Magazine

*"*Setting Up Your Shots *is a great book for defining the shots of today. The storyboard examples on every page make it a valuable reference book for directors and DPs alike! This great learning tool should be a boon for writers who want to choose the most effective shot and clearly show it in their boards for the maximum impact."*
— Paul Clatworthy, Creator, StoryBoard Artist and StoryBoard Quick Software

"This book is for both beginning and experienced filmmakers. It's a great reference tool, a quick reminder of the most commonly used shots by the greatest filmmakers of all time."
— Cory Williams, President, Alternative Productions

JEREMY VINEYARD is a filmmaker, internationally published author, and screenwriter. He is currently assembling a cast and crew for a crime feature to be shot in 2005.

$19.95 | 132 PAGES | ORDER # 8RLS | ISBN: 0-941188-73-6

MICHAEL WIESE PRODUCTIONS

Since 1981, Michael Wiese Productions has been dedicated to providing both novice and seasoned filmmakers with vital information on all aspects of filmmaking. We have published more than 70 books, used in over 500 film schools and countless universities, and by hundreds of thousands of filmmakers worldwide.

Our authors are successful industry professionals who spend innumerable hours writing about the hard stuff: budgeting, financing, directing, marketing, and distribution. They believe that if they share their knowledge and experience with others, more high quality films will be produced.

And that has been our mission, now complemented through our new web-based resources. We invite all readers to visit www.mwp.com to receive free tipsheets and sample chapters, participate in forum discussions, obtain product discounts — and even get the opportunity to receive free books, project consulting, and other services offered by our company.

Our goal is, quite simply, to help you reach your goals. That's why we give our readers the most complete portal for filmmaking knowledge available — in the most convenient manner.

We truly hope that our books and web-based resources will empower you to create enduring films that will last for generations to come.

Let us hear from you at anytime.

Sincerely,
Michael Wiese
Publisher, Filmmaker

www.mwp.com

FILM & VIDEO BOOKS

Alone In a Room: *Secrets of Successful Screenwriters*
John Scott Lewinski / $19.95

Cinematic Storytelling: *The 100 Most Powerful Film Conventions Every Filmmaker Must Know* / Jennifer Van Sijll / $22.95

The Complete Independent Movie Marketing Handbook: *Promote, Distribute & Sell Your Film or Video* / Mark Steven Bosko / $39.95

Costume Design 101: *The Art and Business of Costume Design for Film and Television* / Richard La Motte / $19.95

Could It Be a Movie? *How to Get Your Ideas Out of Your Head and Up on the Screen* / Christina Hamlett / $26.95

Crashing Hollywood: *How to Keep Your Integrity Up, Your Clothes On & Still Make It in Hollywood* / Fran Harris / $24.95

Creating Characters: *Let Them Whisper Their Secrets*
Marisa D'Vari / $26.95

The Crime Writer's Reference Guide: *1001 Tips for Writing the Perfect Murder*
Martin Roth / $17.95

Cut by Cut: *Editing Your Film or Video*
Gael Chandler / $35.95

Cut to the Chase: *Forty-Five Years of Editing America's Favorite Movies*
Sam O'Steen as told to Bobbie O'Steen / $24.95

Digital Cinema: *The Hollywood Insider's Guide to the Evolution of Storytelling*
Thom Taylor and Melinda Hsu / $27.95

Digital Editing with Final Cut Pro 4 *(includes 45 minutes of DVD tutorials and sample footage)* / Bruce Mamer and Jason Wallace / $31.95

Digital Filmmaking 101: *An Essential Guide to Producing Low-Budget Movies*
Dale Newton and John Gaspard / $24.95

Digital Moviemaking, 2nd Edition: *All the Skills, Techniques, and Moxie You'll Need to Turn Your Passion into a Career* / Scott Billups / $26.95

Directing Actors: *Creating Memorable Performances for Film and Television*
Judith Weston / $26.95

Directing Feature Films: *The Creative Collaboration Between Directors, Writers, and Actors* / Mark Travis / $26.95

Dream Gear: *Cool & Innovative Tools for Film, Video & TV Professionals*
Catherine Lorenze / $29.95

The Encyclopedia of Underground Movies: *Films from the Fringes of Cinema*
Phil Hall / $26.95

The Eye is Quicker *Film Editing: Making a Good Film Better*
Richard D. Pepperman / $27.95

Film & Video Budgets, 3rd Updated Edition
Deke Simon and Michael Wiese / $26.95

Film Directing: Cinematic Motion, 2nd Edition
Steven D. Katz / $27.95

Film Directing: Shot by Shot, *Visualizing from Concept to Screen*
Steven D. Katz / $27.95

The Film Director's Intuition: *Script Analysis and Rehearsal Techniques*
Judith Weston / $26.95

Film Production Management 101: *The Ultimate Guide for Film and Television Production Management and Coordination* / Deborah S. Patz / $39.95

Filmmaking for Teens: *Pulling Off Your Shorts*
Troy Lanier and Clay Nichols / $18.95

First Time Director: *How to Make Your Breakthrough Movie*
Gil Bettman / $27.95

From Word to Image: *Storyboarding and the Filmmaking Process*
Marcie Begleiter / $26.95

The Hollywood Standard: *The Complete & Authoritative Guide to Script Format and Style* / Christopher Riley / $18.95

The Independent Film and Videomakers Guide, 2nd Edition: *Expanded and Updated* / Michael Wiese / $29.95

Inner Drives: *How to Write & Create Characters Using the Eight Classic Centers of Motivation* / Pamela Jaye Smith / $26.95

Joe Leydon's Guide to Essential Movies You Must See: *If You Read, Write About – or Make Movies* / Joe Leydon / $24.95

Myth and the Movies: *Discovering the Mythic Structure of 50 Unforgettable Films* / Stuart Voytilla / $26.95

On the Edge of a Dream: *Magic & Madness in Bali*
Michael Wiese / $16.95

The Perfect Pitch: *How to Sell Yourself and Your Movie Idea to Hollywood*
Ken Rotcop / $16.95

Psychology for Screenwriters: *Building Conflict in your Script*
William Indick, Ph.D. / $26.95

Save the Cat! *The Last Book on Screenwriting You'll Ever Need*
Blake Snyder / $19.95

Screenwriting 101: *The Essential Craft of Feature Film Writing*
Neill D. Hicks / $16.95

Script Partners: *What Makes Film and TV Writing Teams Work*
Claudia Johnson and Matt Stevens / $24.95

The Script-Selling Game: *A Hollywood Insider's Look at Getting Your Script Sold and Produced* / Kathie Fong Yoneda / $14.95

Setting Up Your Shots: *Great Camera Moves Every Filmmaker Should Know*
Jeremy Vineyard / $19.95

Shaking the Money Tree, 2nd Edition: *How to Get Grants and Donations for Film and Television* / Morrie Warshawski / $26.95

Sound Design: *The Expressive Power of Music, Voice, and Sound Effects in Cinema* / David Sonnenschein / $19.95

Stealing Fire From the Gods: *A Dynamic New Story Model for Writers and Filmmakers* / James Bonnet / $26.95

Storyboarding 101: *A Crash Course in Professional Storyboarding*
James O. Fraioli / $19.95

The Ultimate Filmmaker's Guide to Short Films: *Making It Big in Shorts*
Kim Adelman / $14.95

What Are You Laughing At? *How to Write Funny Screenplays, Stories, and More* / Brad Schreiber / $19.95

The Working Director: *How to Arrive, Thrive & Survive in the Director's Chair*
Charles Wilkinson / $22.95

The Writer's Journey, 2nd Edition: *Mythic Structure for Writers*
Christopher Vogler / $24.95

The Writer's Partner: *1001 Breakthrough Ideas to Stimulate Your Imagination*
Martin Roth / $19.95

Writing the Action Adventure: *The Moment of Truth*
Neill D. Hicks / $14.95

Writing the Comedy Film: *Make 'Em Laugh*
Stuart Voytilla and Scott Petri / $14.95

Writing the Fantasy Film: *Heroes and Journeys in Alternate Realities*
Sable Jak / $26.95

Writing the Killer Treatment: *Selling Your Story Without a Script*
Michael Halperin / $14.95

Writing the Second Act: *Building Conflict and Tension in Your Film Script*
Michael Halperin / $19.95

Writing the Thriller Film: *The Terror Within*
Neill D. Hicks / $14.95

DVD & VIDEOS

Hardware Wars: *DVD*
Written and Directed by Ernie Fosselius / $14.95

Hardware Wars: *Special Edition VHS Video*
Written and Directed by Ernie Fosselius / $9.95

Field of Fish: *VHS Video*
Directed by Steve Tanner and Michael Wiese, Written by Annamaria Murphy / $9.95